# DESERT STORM

## Kurt Warner and the Arizona Cardinals' Unforgettable Run to the Super Bowl

TRIUMPH
BOOKS

Larry Fitzgerald sprints for the end zone on his 64-yard touchdown catch to give the Cardinals their first lead of the game with 2:47 to go in the fourth quarter of Super Bowl XLIII.

This book is available in quantity at special discounts for your group
or organization. For further information, contact:

**Triumph Books**
542 South Dearborn Street
Suite 750
Chicago, Illinois 60605
(312) 939-3330
Fax (312) 663-3557

Printed in United States of America
ISBN: 978-1-60078-305-0

Photos courtesy of AP Images except where otherwise indicated

**Content packaged by Mojo Media, Inc.**
Joe Funk: Editor
Jason Hinman: Creative Director

# contents

Introduction ................................................. 6

Super Bowl XLIII ........................................ 10

NFC Playoffs .............................................. 16

2008 Cardinals Preseason ........................... 30

Regular Season ........................................... 34

Kurt Warner: The Early Years ..................... 98

Kurt Warner NFL Stats ............................... 126

# Introduction

While Arizona Cardinals' fans went into 2008 with a sense of optimism, a rare commodity among followers of this much-maligned franchise, very few people would have predicted the amazing season that followed. Though 2007's 8–8 record and the team's improved focus under head coach Ken Whisenhunt—a product of the Steelers' championship factory—had Cardinals followers thinking postseason (seemingly off-limits to the team since the Clinton administration) a trip to the Super Bowl seemed pure fantasy.

As training camp opened in the summer of 2008, not all signs were positive. A full-blown quarterback controversy grabbed headlines even before a single preseason game had been played. Would Ken Whisenhunt stick with his appointed starter, Matt Leinart, or was aging legend Kurt Warner still a better bet? What about star receiver, Anquan Boldin, who was not shy about his desire to be traded? And was there enough new talent from what appeared to be a lackluster draft class to push Arizona into the postseason?

These questions were soon answered, but the 2008 season was nonetheless a wild ride for Arizona faithful, punctuated by an up-and-down start that left everyone wondering just how good—or bad—this team was; a three-week winning streak over division foes that put the team in the driver's seat for an NFC West title; and a 2–4 coast into the postseason that earned the Cardinals the dubious label as the weakest club in the playoffs. Yes, Arizona had reached the playoffs, but the team had failed to make much of an impression on anybody. One-and-done was the consensus.

But ultimately, Ken Whisenhunt, Kurt Warner, and a host of other Cardinals rewarded fans with a postseason run for the ages, dominating three favored NFC foes and coming within a tip-toe of beating the Steelers in the Super Bowl. They may have lost the final game, but the Cardinals won the hearts of Arizona fans, and made believers out of the rest of the league—this was one exceptional team.

---

The buildup to Arizona's appearance in Super Bowl XLIII officially started four years earlier with the signing of Kurt Warner—the first of two significant events that helped turn the Cardinals into a winning team. Warner, a two-time MVP, had led the Rams to two Super Bowls and one championship, but was coming off a forgettable one-year stint with the Giants during which he gave way to the up-and-coming Eli Manning. Arizona offered

Ever since he arrived in Arizona and unseated Matt Leinart in the starting lineup, Warner has pointed the Cardinals in the right direction.

Warner a one-year deal, he out-dueled Josh McCown for the starting job, and he was rewarded with a new three-year contract. Nonetheless, most observers thought the veteran was back in the "caretaker" role he filled in New York, holding the job only until whatever big-name quarterback Arizona was expected to take in the 2006 draft was ready to take over the job.

The "big name' turned out to be USC's Matt Leinart, delivered to the desert with a No. 10 pick in 2006's first round. Many observers thought Leinart was a sure bet to beat out old man Warner for the signal-caller's job to start his rookie year, but a contract holdout kept Leinart off the field for much of the preseason. Leinart remained on the bench behind Warner to start the regular season, but the rookie was starting by the sixth game. For Warner, it appeared that a repeat of his New York experience was in the works.

When head coach Dennis Green was fired after the 2006 season, the stage was set for the second significant event in the Cardinals' revival. On January 14, 2007, Ken Whisenhunt was hired to replace Green, a development that shocked many across the league. Whisenhunt had been the offensive coordinator for the Pittsburgh Steelers—only a year removed from their latest Super Bowl victory—and his boss and mentor, Bill Cowher, had just announced his retirement. To many, Whisenhunt's ascendancy to the top job in Pittsburgh seemed a foregone conclusion. But when the Steelers interviewed Whisenhunt and failed to make him an offer, Arizona pounced. Whisenhunt took the sure thing in the desert and became the Cards' head coach.

Whisenhunt brought a focus and a discipline that had been lacking in Arizona for years, and his positive impact on the team could be seen right from the start. And while many optimists predicted instant success, there was a lot of work to be done. The quarterback position proved particularly problematic, as Leinart struggled before being injured and lost for the year. Whisenhunt turned to Warner to steady the team, and he delivered, looking a lot more like an MVP than a backup by the end of the season. With Warner leading the way, the Cardinals stayed in the playoff hunt until late in the year and finished a respectable 8–8.

For many NFL franchises, a .500 record is reason for wringing hands and firing assistant coaches, but for the Cardinals it was affirmation that the team was on the right track. And as Ken Whisenhunt looked back on his opening campaign, and weighed tough questions (like which starting quarterback would give the team the best chance for winning now), he must have felt optimistic. And though—even privately—he might not have been ready to predict a trip to Tampa, he must have had an inkling that the 2008 season was going to be an unforgettable one in Arizona. ∎

With Christian convictions and professional prowess, Warner arrived in the desert and nearly led his team to the promised land in his first full year as starter.

# Super Bowl XLIII

## Standing Tall Through it All

Most fans around the country didn't believe in them. Most fans in the stadium at Super Bowl XLIII didn't believe in them.

Here they were, the Arizona Cardinals, with a losing tradition comparable perhaps only to the Chicago Cubs, only one win from a world championship.

But Kurt Warner believed. So did his coach, Ken Whisenhunt. And backed by a group of teammates and an organization anxious to shed a culture of losing, the Cardinals almost pulled off an upset against the Pittsburgh Steelers, one of the most successful franchises in pro sports.

Warner was confident heading into the big game. After a fine season that catapulted him back among the league's elite NFL quarterbacks, he was making his third Super Bowl appearance. A championship-winner once before, Warner had played in two of the most exciting Super Bowls of all time with the St. Louis Rams, games in which he had recorded the first and second most passing yards in Super Bowl history.

Years removed from his days with "The Greatest Show on Turf," Warner relished the chance to go for another ring. "To come back here when everybody counted us out, when everybody counted me out, when everybody told us every single week, 'Well, the Cardinals don't have a chance against Atlanta, they definitely don't have a chance against Carolina, and they really don't have a chance against Philadelphia,' and then you accomplish that, it's really, really special," he said of the Cardinals' three playoff wins in the days leading up to the Super Bowl.

Despite their resolve, the championship game against the favored Steelers started poorly for the Cardinals. After taking the opening kickoff, Pittsburgh marched down the field. On third and goal from the 1-yard line, it looked like Pittsburgh had scored after Ben Roethlisberger called his own number and charged towards the goal line. But a replay challenge from Ken Whisenhunt reversed the touchdown call on the field and forced Pittsburgh to settle for an 18-yard field goal from Jeff Reed.

Arizona continued to misfire through the rest of the first quarter as the Steelers controlled the clock, though the Cardinals only trailed by three after the first 15 minutes.

With the Cardinals stuck in first gear, Pittsburgh extended its lead just one minute into the second quarter. Running back Gary Russell followed the blocking of his right guard and right tackle and tumbled into the end zone from one yard out to make the score 10–0.

With 9:30 in the second quarter, Warner and

With a proven record of playing well in big games, Captain Kurt made sure his teammates were ready to play and would not be intimidated on sports' biggest stage. He also demonstrated his leadership by completing 31 of 43 passes for 377 yards, three touchdowns, and one pick.

the Cardinals settled down and pieced together a scoring drive to cut into the Pittsburgh lead. The key play saw Warner connecting on his first long pass of the game, a 45-yard completion to Anquan Boldin that took Arizona to the Pittsburgh 1-yard line. Warner nearly fell over taking the snap on the next play, but managed to regain his balance and hit Ben Patrick for a touchdown to shave the Steelers' lead to three points.

Though the remainder of the second quarter was somewhat uneventful, Arizona threatened to turn the game upside-down as halftime neared. Cardinals outside linebacker Karlos Dansby intercepted a tipped Ben Roethlisberger pass and gave the Cardinals possession at the Steelers' 34 with two timeouts and 2:00 left. The Steelers made the Cardinals work for their yardage, but Arizona was just inches from the go-ahead touchdown and working with 18 seconds on the clock when Warner made an uncharacteristic miscalculation. He read the defense, looked left, and fired a slant pass to Boldin—but it never got to him.

Though he had read what he thought was a blitz by Pittsburgh linebacker James Harrison, Warner realized a split second after he released the ball that Harrison had fallen back into coverage. Harrison deftly intercepted the ball at the goal line and trucked 100 yards down the sideline for a touchdown, falling into the end zone on top of Larry Fitzgerald after time on the clock had expired, swinging the score to 17–7 and the momentum back to the Steelers. It was the longest play in Super Bowl history and surely one of the most amazing. Warner said afterwards of the pivotal play: "I knew the blitz was coming. He (Harrison) faked like he was coming, but I couldn't see over the top of my linemen...so I thought I had a crease for Anquan. I tried to throw it in there. But James popped out and did a great job of not only making the catch but a tremendous job on the return after that."

Down by 10 points and stung by an unlikely play, the Cardinals would have to overcome adversity and slow down the rolling Steelers. And once again, as they had all season, Arizona would rise to the occasion—but the second half did not start the way they hoped. Looking to take control of the game and burn clock, the Steelers mounted a long, time-consuming drive, capitalizing on three personal fouls by the Cardinals. The drive ended with Jeff Reed's second chip-shot field goal of the game to stretch the Pittsburgh lead to 20–7.

Down by two scores with just 15 minutes to go in the Super Bowl, Warner and the comeback Cardinals finally had the Steelers where they wanted them.

Switching to the no-huddle offense in the fourth quarter, the Cardinals closed the gap to 20–14 thanks to an eight play, 87-yard pass-and-catch clinic. Warner capped the drive by floating a pass over Pittsburgh's Ike Taylor and into the hands of his all-world clutch receiver, Larry Fitzgerald.

After pinning the Steelers deep with a well-placed punt, the Cardinals forced Pittsburgh into committing a holding penalty in the end zone, resulting in a safety. Now trailing by four with 2:58 remaining, plenty of time for Warner, the

Willie Parker looks but finds little daylight against safeties Adrian Wilson and Antrel Rolle in the third quarter. The Cardinals defense played well, holding Parker to 53 yards and the Steelers team to just 58 rushing yards and 234 passing yards.

Cardinals were poised to take the lead.

Following the free kick, it only took Arizona two plays to find the end zone. Warner summoned his late-game magic one more time and found a streaking Fitzgerald over the middle for a 64-yard touchdown that put Arizona in front 23–20—the Cardinals' first lead of the game.

The Steelers had just 2:37 to come back, but that was more than enough time for Ben Roethlisberger, who improvised on almost every play as he took his team down the field. With less than a minute to play, Roethlisberger lofted a pass to the corner of the end zone, connecting with game-MVP Santonio Holmes, who snagged the ball and dragged his toes on the turf to make the score 27–23.

But there were still 35 seconds left, Arizona had two timeouts, and with Warner at quarterback they had a glimmer of hope. With 22 seconds to play, Warner had moved the Cardinals out past their 40, and they crossed midfield with 15 seconds left. On the next play, however, Warner stepped up to throw and was stripped of the ball as he cocked his arm for release. The Steelers pounced on the loose ball, and the Cardinals' dreams of Super Bowl glory were over.

Despite the loss, the 2008-2009 Cardinals had a great run, performed admirably on the NFL's biggest stage, and Kurt Warner had another day for the ages, finishing 31-of-43 for 377 yards, three touchdowns, and that one, historic interception.

And while the loss clearly hurt him and everyone in the Cardinals dressing room, the classy Warner was still gracious in defeat. "These guys

have exceeded expectations. I am proud," Warner said. "We gave ourselves a chance to win a world championship, but that other team went out and won it. I give them a whole bunch of credit, but I am glad to be on this sideline with this Cardinals team and organization." ∎

Kurt Warner's biggest fan, his wife Brenda, was there to support her husband as she has since his days as a grocery bagger in Iowa.

# Team Stats

|  | PIT | ARI |
|---|---|---|
| **First Downs** | 20 | 23 |
| Passing | 12 | 20 |
| Rushing | 4 | 2 |
| Penalty | 4 | 1 |
| **Third Down Efficiency** | 4-10 | 3-8 |
| **Fourth Down Efficiency** | 0-0 | 0-0 |
| **TOTAL NET YARDS** | 292 | 407 |
| Total Plays | 58 | 57 |
| Average Gain Per Play | 5.0 | 7.1 |
| **NET YARDS RUSHING** | 58 | 33 |
| Rushes | 26 | 12 |
| Average Per Rush | 2.2 | 2.8 |
| **NET YARDS PASSING** | 234 | 374 |
| Completions-Attempts | 21-30 | 31-43 |
| Yards Per Pass Play | 7.3 | 8.3 |
| Times Sacked | 2 | 2 |
| Yards Lost to Sacks | 22 | 3 |
| Had Intercepted | 1 | 1 |
| **PUNTS** | 3 | 5 |
| Average Punt | 46.3 | 36.0 |
| **PENALTIES** | 7 | 11 |
| Penalty Yards | 56 | 106 |
| **FUMBLES** | 0 | 2 |
| Fumbles Lost | 0 | 1 |
| TIME OF POSSESSION | 33:01 | 26:59 |

# NFC Playoffs

## The Cardinals rose above every challenge in their remarkable postseason run

Forget the MVPs. Forget the Super Bowls. Forget one of the greatest rags-to-riches stories in the history of sports. Kurt Warner may have punched his ticket to Canton during an eight-minute span of the NFC Championship Game against Philadelphia. Showing amazing calm and delivering pin-point-accurate passes, the 37-year-old quarterback led his team on a 14-play, 72-yard drive that was darn near "Elway-esque" in execution. Warner's brilliant march to paydirt delivered a 32–25 victory over the Eagles and an unlikely Super Bowl berth for the Arizona Cardinals, one of pro sports' most under-achieving franchises.

The Cardinals' journey to Tampa began with a long, physical slog beneath the klieg lights and amid the cascading shrieks of University of Phoenix Stadium. For almost an hour it went on in real time, numerals winking off the clock, pads clashing, the white helmets scored with green, and the green with white, the battle-scarred turf a testimony to the contest's brutality.

The Cardinals had soared to a 24–6 advantage in the first half starting with an 80-yard touchdown drive to open the game and including a flea flicker from Warner to Larry Fitzgerald that netted 62 yards on a "Philly Special." Only their vaunted defenders had kept the Eagles in the game.

Trailing Arizona by 18 points at the half, the Eagles had stormed back in the third quarter with 19 unanswered points. In slightly more than eight minutes, quarterback Donovan McNabb had completed 13 of 19 passes for 223 yards and three touchdowns, the third a 62-yard arc and juggling catch by rookie DeSean Jackson to give Philadelphia its first lead of the game at 25–24 with less than 11 minutes left to play.

Now, as they gathered around Warner following the ensuing kickoff, the Cardinals found themselves 72 yards from six points, and 40 to 50 yards from an attempt at three. Anything less more than likely spelled doom. The Cardinals knew it, the Eagles knew it, and from the rumble of unease now coursing the stadium, the crowd knew it. "You could see the look in the guys' eyes," Fitzgerald said of his teammates. "Nobody wanted to let the team down."

The now-historic drive began inauspiciously. On first down, Edgar James lost a yard off left tackle—leaving the Cardinals 73 yards from the end zone. Kurt Warner, who'd been in a lot tougher places during his life, wasn't fazed. He hooked up with Fitzgerald for the receiver's first catch of the second half, moving the Cards 15 yards to their own 42, then connected with Leonard Pope for nine yards to break into Eagles' territory. When Edgerrin

*Kurt Warner celebrates with fans after engineering the Cardinals' drive into history.*

James lost a yard and Tim Hightower got it back—plus a little more—on the next two plays, the chains were called in to see if Arizona had earned a first down. The verdict? Fourth and inches.

The Eagles crowded the line, expecting Arizona to power up the middle, but they responded with what seemed an odd call: a slow-developing sweep to the right by Tim Hightower. The 224-pound rookie methodically worked his way toward the sideline and when an opening appeared, he turned

## The Cardinals' Drive: 14 Plays to Greatness

**1: 1st and 10, ARI 28 (10:39)**
James off left tackle for -1 yard

**2: 2nd and 11, ARI 27 (10:00)**
Warner pass to Fitzgerald for 15 yards

**3: 1st and 10, ARI 42 (9:24)**
Warner pass to Pope for 9 yards

**4: 2nd and 1, PHI 49 (8:47)**
James up the middle for -1 yard

**5: 3rd and 2, 50 (8:03)**
Hightower off left tackle for 1 yard

**6: 4th and 1, PHI 49 (7:57)**
Hightower around the right end for 6 yards

**7: 1st and 10, PHI 43 (7:21)**
James up the middle for 2 yards

**8: 2nd and 8, PHI 41 (6:36)**
Warner pass to Fitzgerald for 18 yards

**9: 1st and 10, PHI 23 (5:52)**
James off right tackle for 3 yards

**10: 2nd and 7, PHI 20 (5:13)**
Warner pass to Fitzgerald for 6 yards

**11: 3rd and 1, PHI 14 (4:26)**
Hightower off right tackle for 5 yards

**12: 1st and goal, PHI 9 (3:44)—**
James up the middle for no gain

**13: 2nd and goal, PHI 9 (3:06)**
Hightower off left tackle for 1 yard

**14: 3rd and goal, PHI 8 (2:59)**
Warner pass to Hightower for 8 yards, TD

the corner and slashed forward for six yards and a first down at the Eagles' 43.

In reality, the play had been designed for Hightower to follow fullback Terrelle Smith into the middle of the line, but at the last instant he broke to the right. "It's a thing where you make a read and kind of take a chance," he would say. "Anytime it's third or fourth and 1, you don't want to run laterally. You want to go north and south as fast as you can. But sometimes you have to take a risk. That's what I did. Fortunately it worked out for the good."

Asked later if the play selection was difficult, Whisenhunt said, "Not since we made it, it wasn't."

On second and 8, Warner hit Fitzgerald for another 18 yards to the Eagles' 23. James sliced off right tackle for three, then Warner returned to Fitzgerald for the wideout's third catch of the drive, moving to the Eagles' 14. On third and 1, Hightower powered over right tackle for first and goal at the 9.

Arizona moved just one yard on its next two plays and a field-goal try was looking likely, but Hightower proved his worth again. On third down, Warner flipped a middle screen to Hightower, who veered right and bulled through two Eagles at the goal line for the touchdown. Unsure of whether the Eagles planned to blitz or not, Warner said the play had been set up so that it didn't matter. Only 2:53 remained in the game.

"I don't think anyone expected it," Hightower said. "It was another of those plays that when they called it, I knew it was going to work. I knew if they put the ball in my hands, I was going to find a way. I don't care what I had to do. The whole team's counting on you, the whole city's counting on you."

Warner completed 61 passes in 92 attempts for eight touchdowns and a 112.1 QB rating in the Cardinals' three playoff wins.

Ken Whisenhunt's ability to rapidly change the decades-old culture of losing in the Cardinals organization may be his most impressive accomplishment of all.

"We brought a lot of our speed screens down there near the end zone," Whisenhunt said. "We've had a great deal of success doing that. So we put in a play off those, and it worked well."

Warner's strike to Ben Patrick on the two-point conversion made it 32–25 Arizona, and a few minutes later, the Cardinals were in the Super Bowl. Of their 72-yard drive to victory, Warner said, "I didn't see any panic. We got into that huddle and I don't think a lot was said. No one was hyperventilating or anything like that. It was, 'Hey, business as usual.'"

Up in the TV booth, broadcaster Joe Buck asked, "You think there's ever been a drive that put a guy into the Hall of Fame?"

Sometime in the next decade or so, we'll know the answer to that question.

———————————

Arizona's playoff run—their first postseason appearance in a decade—had started two weeks earlier on this same field. The Cardinals were hosting the game as a division champ, but their 9–7 record and anemic late-season play had the visiting Atlanta Falcons a decided favorite despite their wild-card status. The "bird team" from the Southeast was one of the NFL's feel-good stories in 2008. Their new GM, coach, starting quarterback, and winning attitude had elevated them from the depths of the league to an 11–5 mark and dreams of a trip to Tampa.

But the experts forgot that the Cardinals had been writing their own success story in 2008, with Warner serving as the primary protagonist, and they were ready for the Falcons. Arizona got down to business in the first quarter when Warner completed a 42-yard touchdown pass to Fitzgerald. He added a 71-yard touchdown strike to Anquan

Boldin in the second (following a Falcon field goal), and Arizona had what appeared to be comfortable 14–3 lead. It wasn't; Arizona yielded two Falcons touchdowns late in the half and went into the locker room down by three.

When Boldin pulled a hamstring on the scoring play, the Cardinals offense seemed to go dormant for a while, but fortunately the defense rescued them from their funk. When Falcons rookie QB Matt Ryan fumbled a handoff on the first possession of the second half, Antrel Rolle scooped up the ball and raced 27 yards for the go-ahead score. Arizona never trailed after that point.

Defensive pressure on Ryan made all the difference. In addition to the fumble, he yielded two picks and was tackled in the end zone for a fourth-quarter safety. The Falcons could muster just one second-half score, a touchdown with 4:19 remaining.

"A lot of people, coming into this game, said we were the worst playoff team ever," head coach Ken Whisenhunt noted after the stirring 30–24 triumph. "We rallied around that."

It was also the franchise's first playoff game at home since the then–Chicago Cardinals defeated the Philadelphia Eagles for the NFL title in 1947.

Everyone knew that the 2008 Cardinals could pass, but a resolute defense and effective running game proved to be the edge. "You have to really give credit first to their defense," said Falcons guard Harvey Dahl. "They did an outstanding job. They were flying all over the place."

"We couldn't run the ball," Falcons wide receiver Roddy White said of his team's 60 yards rushing, a season low. "We had to throw it around a little bit more than we're used to. Things like that put us behind the 8-ball."

Edgerrin James carried 16 times for 73 yards,

*It was a special treat for the Cardinals and their fans to clinch their first-ever trip to a Super Bowl at home.*

outgaining Atlanta's Michael Turner—the NFL's second-leading rusher with 1,699 yards on the season—who managed just 42 yards in 18 carries.

It was Warner's first playoff game since he led the Rams to the Super Bowl in 2001 and he performed well in the postseason spotlight, completing 19 of 32 passes for 271 yards. "I hope this gives us a lot of confidence," he said. "We thought we could win this game, and hopefully we can parlay this into more confidence and know we can win wherever we have to go."

When the game was over, Whisenhunt jogged along the front row of seats, high-fiving Cardinals

fans. The game had not been sold out until Friday, but the capacity crowd of 72,650 roared enthusiastically after the victory.

Next for Arizona was a stiff road test against the Carolina Panthers. The Cardinals entered the contest as a 10-point underdog; critics were quick to point out their 0–5 record in the Eastern time zone this season. Arizona had been embarrassed when it ventured far from home, but the closest it came was a 27–23 loss at Charlotte in October when the Cardinals blew a two-touchdown lead.

(above) Steve Breaston continued to be a factor in the playoffs following a sophomore season where he posted 77 catches for 1,006 yards and three touchdowns. (opposite) Larry Fitzgerald snares a touchdown over the Atlanta Falcons' Lawyer Milloy (36) and Chris Houston (23) in the NFC wild-card playoff game. Fitzgerald caught six passes for 101 yards and a touchdown.

The reemergence of Edgerrin James and the running game came along just in time to help fuel the Cardinals' playoff run. James rushed 52 times for 203 yards and a touchdown in three playoff games.

There would be no suspense this time.

Entering with a 5–2 postseason record, Panthers QB Jake Delhomme's 95.0 playoff passer rating was better than any other quarterback participating in the 2008 postseason. But Delhomme threw two interceptions and lost a fumble in the first half, making things easy for the Cardinals. Defensive end Antonio Smith stripped Delhomme and recovered the ball at the Carolina 13 late in the first quarter. Two plays later, Edgerrin James' 4-yard touchdown run put the Cardinals ahead to stay at 14–7. While Anquan Boldin sat out—the victim of a hamstring pull suffered catching a long TD against Atlanta—Larry Fitzgerald more than made up for the loss. The lanky receiver set a team playoff record for receiving yards (166), making it look easy against the Panthers' secondary.

Kurt Warner's conversion of a second-quarter Delhomme pick into a touchdown pass to Larry Fitzgerald led to a 27–7 halftime lead for Arizona that left the Carolina crowd silent. Things weren't much better for the home team in the second half and the Cardinals cruised to a relatively easy 33–13 win over the Panthers—the league's only unbeaten team at home during the regular season.

"We didn't do anything, and you know before you go on the field that if you don't play well, you are going home," said Panthers defensive end Julius Peppers. "It didn't happen for us today and we've got a long time to think about it."

Just shy of the NFL playoff record for interceptions, Delhomme became the first player to have five picks in a postseason game since Oakland quarterback Rich Gannon's disastrous appearance in the 2003 Super Bowl. "I'm at a loss for words," Delhomme said. "Usually I'm not. For one reason or another, I didn't give us a chance tonight."

Though Delhomme's interceptions paralyzed Carolina's passing attack, the Cardinals' stingy run defense played a huge role in the win—DeAngelo Williams was held to just 63 yards on the ground. It was a crushing loss for the Panthers, the No. 2 seed in the NFC. "We picked a bad day to have a bad day," coach John Fox said

A team that had won only two playoff games in their history before defeating Atlanta, the Cardinals became the last NFC team to reach a conference championship since the 1970 merger of the NFL and AFL. Kurt Warner led the charge again, tossing two more touchdown passes and acting like this postseason business was old hat for him.

"It's a group of guys that put their mind to going out and playing great football," said Warner, who completed 21 of 32 passes for 220 yards. Only one interception marred his outstanding performance. "Everybody that needed to step up, stepped up. Everybody that needed to make a play, made a play and that's what it's all about."

Ken Whisenhunt acknowledged that criticism of his team may have fueled their fire to win. "Not many people had very nice things to say about us and didn't give us a chance," said the second-year coach who seems to be turning around the losing culture of the Cardinals' franchise. "I think we've showed we can come to the East Coast and win a game. We believe in ourselves. I like being the underdog, and we're going to continue to be the underdog." ■

A suddenly stubborn Cardinals defense harassed Jake Delhomme all day and forced the veteran quarterback into five interceptions.

# 2008 Cardinals Preseason

## QB Controversy Dominates the Headlines

The roots of the Arizona Cardinals' Super Bowl season can be traced back to January 2008. The Cards were coming off a tantalizing 8–8 campaign in which they flirted with the playoffs but came up short. Though it was just Ken Whisenhunt's first season as head coach, the former Steelers' coordinator had initiated a culture change that finally had Arizona fans conjuring championship dreams. Yet the Cardinals' head man had a major hurdle to clear in his quest to build a winning team: choose a starting quarterback.

Going into the 2007 campaign, it appeared that former first-round draft pick Matt Leinart was the man destined to lead the Cardinals for the next several seasons. Also on the roster was former MVP Kurt Warner, whose first two forgettable seasons in the desert had many observers convinced his storybook career was approaching its end. Then the unexpected happened: Leinart played poorly and ultimately found himself on injured reserve thanks to a broken collarbone. Warner assumed the starter's role, threw 27 touchdown passes, and rediscovered some of his old magic in keeping the Cards in the playoff hunt.

So after the season, Whisenhunt made a logical move—he named Leinart the starter for 2008. And why not? With only 16 games as a starter under his belt, it was too early to write off the Cardinals' quarterback of the future—especially when he had been forced to vacate the job because of an injury.

With that decision behind him, Whisenhunt and rest of the Arizona brain trust turned their attention to the draft. Fans hoping for a quick fix going into the 2008 season were probably disappointed with the Cardinals' list of picks, which included three players from Football Championship Subdivision schools. Ultimately, all three of the small-school players made the 2008 squad, and two emerged as standouts in the team's playoff run. First-round pick Dominique Rogers-Cromartie, a cornerback out of Tennessee State, worked his way into the starting lineup and finished the regular season with 42 tackles and 4 interceptions. On the offensive side, fifth-round pick Tim Hightower, a running back from Richmond, rushed for 399 yards and 10 touchdowns serving as the team's power-running No. 2 back.

As training camp opened, interest in the rookies was secondary to curiosity about the looming quarterback battle. Despite Whisenhunt's pronouncement

The Cardinals quarterbacks run drills during training camp. All four made the team, though Tyler Palko (back) was kept on the practice squad.

Everything was turned upside-down the next week during the Cardinals' 24–0 victory over the Raiders. Leinart, opening the game as Arizona's QB, looked horrible in throwing three interceptions during an outing in which he completed only 4 of 12 passes for 24 yards. Warner came on in relief and looked shaky on his first drive, but he eventually settled down and led the Cardinals to the victory. Had he earned the No. 1 job?

Warner started the final preseason game against the Broncos and looked good during a brief outing, but Leinart gave Ken Whisenhunt something to think about with his own nice performance. Admittedly, the talent on the field may not have been first-string caliber, but Leinart completed 10 of 14 passes for 177 yards and a touchdown. Who was going to be taking snaps in the regular-season opener in San Francisco?

Surprising many, head coach Ken Whisenhunt picked the 37-year-old Warner. Whisenhunt admitted the decision was not an easy one, and he declined to offer specific reasons for making the call, but it was Warner who probably best summed up why he won the job. "You also realize in this business…you want to win now, and who's going to give us that best chance to win now."

Matt Leinart will get his chance someday, but Cardinals fans are thankful that Ken Whisenhunt picked the right man for 2008. ∎

the previous winter, starter Leinart couldn't help but look over his shoulder—especially when backup Kurt Warner had reminded people at the end of 2007 why he had twice been named league MVP. But going into the first preseason game, Whisenhunt was expressing complete confidence in his young starter. "Matt has done so well in camp and made progress," Whisenhunt gushed.

Leinart responded with a solid performance in the preseason opener against the Saints. He completed 7 of 8 passes for 91 yards in a 15-play stint. Warner stayed on the bench, something Whisenhunt hinted might happen before the game.

In preseason Game 2 against the Chiefs, Warner got the start, stuck around for two series, and looked solid in completing 6-of-9 for 54 yards and a TD to Larry Fitzgerald. Leinart came on in relief and the team responded with a trio of three-and-outs, before he finally led them on a nice scoring drive to open the second half. His final numbers were solid and his hold on the starting job seemed secure.

(opposite) The teacher and the student. Pushed to the back burner to allow Matt Leinart a chance to start in 2006, Kurt Warner re-asserted himself as a top-tier NFL starter in 2008. (above) Warner has been gracious in the past when Leinart takes the snaps.

# Game 1

## New faces in new places result in unsightly win

The Arizona Cardinals and the San Francisco 49ers both entered the 2008 regular season opener with different starting quarterbacks from their 2007 openers. Fortunately for the Cardinals, their "new" starter was former MVP Kurt Warner, while the 49ers had journeyman J.T. O'Sullivan taking the snaps. Though in most other respects the teams matched up evenly, it was the critical QB position that made all the difference. Veteran Warner proved steady, never turning the ball over and completing 19 of 30 passes for 197 yards. O'Sullivan, on the other hand, melted under Arizona's defensive pressure and yielded two lost fumbles and a pick. In all, the Cardinals recorded five takeaways en route to a 23–13 victory.

Those takeaways proved critical in earning the win, because the Cardinals offense was not yet in sync, and Warner admitted he didn't feel comfortable in the first half. Despite his misgivings, the QB and his offense did enough to go into the locker room tied at 10.

The game turned in the second half. After a nice Arizona drive stalled and led to a short Neil Rackers field goal, a huge hit by Darnell Docket produced one of the O'Sullivan fumbles on the ensuing 49ers' possession. Eight plays later, rookie

Tim Hightower was in the end zone and the score was 20–10.

From there the Cardinals—with the calm Warner now in full control—put on a clinic in ball control, including a 10-minute drive in the fourth quarter that led to a game-icing field goal.

Was this a pretty win? No—the Cardinals should have taken better advantage of the 49ers turnovers and put more points on the board. But the defense was hard-hitting and opportunistic and the offense steady and error-free. Performances like this, especially on the road, are the trademark of playoff-bound teams. Could this be the year...

### Monster Park (San Francisco, Calif.)

| Final | 1 | 2 | 3 | 4 | T |
|---|---|---|---|---|---|
| Arizona (1-0-0) | 3 | 7 | 10 | 3 | 23 |
| San Francisco (0-1-0) | 7 | 3 | 0 | 3 | 13 |

**Game Leaders**

ARI - Pass: K. Warner (19-30, 197), Rush: E. James (26-100)
SF - Pass: J. O'Sullivan (14-20, 195), Rush: F. Gore (14-96)

Adrian Wilson shoves 49ers quarterback J.T. O'Sullivan out of bounds. O'Sullivan passed for 195 yards in his first NFL start, but fumbled the ball away twice.

Kurt Warner and the Cardinals' offense struggled at times, but produced three long, effective scoring drives. Warner completed 19 of 30 passes for 197 yards and a touchdown.

# Game 2

## Warner and Boldin hook up for a command performance

Two wins, no losses. For many NFL franchises, a 2–0 start is such a regular thing that anything less starts fans grumbling and sportswriters raising questions about coaching job security. But in Arizona, 2–0 in 2008 provided a reason to celebrate because it was the first time in 17 seasons that the club won its first two regular-season games. Even sweeter, the game was a rout, with the Cardinals pummeling the visiting Dolphins 31–10.

The 63,445 fans at the University of Phoenix Stadium had barely settled into their seats when the Cardinals turned the game into a runaway. On their first offensive play, Kurt Warner connected with Anquan Boldin for a 79-yard touchdown pass. Later in the quarter, the same pair hooked up on a 3-yard scoring toss. Arizona stretched its lead to 17–0 by halftime.

Quarter three offered more of the same, two long drives capped by touchdowns sandwiched around one Miami field goal. With the Cardinals up 31–3, the last 15 minutes of the game were academic, and Arizona was on its way to a big win.

Kurt Warner was masterful on the day, recording a perfect passer rating of 158.3 for the third time in his career. His line: 19 completions, 24 attempts, 361 yards, three touchdowns, no inter-

ceptions. Just as impressive was Arizona's tandem of talented wideouts. Boldin was on the receiving end of all three Warner TD tosses and caught six balls for 140 yards. Larry Fitzgerald never made it into the end zone, but also recorded six catches for an eye-popping 153 yards.

After the game, coach Ken Whisenhunt tried to keep things cool in the desert. "We did what we were supposed to do today," was how he summarized the game.

Simple task, yes, but one that had eluded the previous 17 Cardinals' teams. ∎

### University of Phoenix Stadium (Glendale, Ariz.)

| Final | 1 | 2 | 3 | 4 | T |
|---|---|---|---|---|---|
| Miami (0-2-0) | 0 | 0 | 3 | 7 | 10 |
| Arizona (2-0-0) | 14 | 3 | 14 | 0 | 31 |

#### Game Leaders

MIA - Pass: C. Pennington (10-20, 112), Rec: D. Hagan (3-51)
ARI - Pass: K. Warner (19-24, 361), Rec: L. Fitzgerald (6-153)

The offensive line did a phenomenal job protecting Kurt Warner against the Dolphins. He responded with a game that harkened back to his MVP years, throwing for 381 yards and three touchdowns—all to Anquan Boldin.

Larry Fitzgerald and the other receivers had plenty of room to operate in the Dolphins' secondary. This acrobatic catch was one of his six receptions that went for a game-high 153 yards.

# Game 3

## Untimely turnovers lead to disappointing day in D.C.

Arizona's dreams of an undefeated season came crashing down on Week 3 at FedEx Field in suburban Washington, D.C. The Cardinals kept the game close but in the end fell to the Redskins 24–17.

Though several factors could be blamed for the loss, one stood out above the others: turnovers. After playing error-free ball in their first two games, the Cardinals yielded two turnovers at critical points in the game. Washington, meanwhile, never gave up the ball and converted the Cardinals' miscues into 10 points.

Arizona lost the ball the first time in the opening quarter while trying to match a Redskins drive that had staked the home team to a 7–0 lead. Edgerrin James' fumble ultimately led to a Washington field goal. The Cardinals' responded more effectively after this second score—a Kurt Warner pass to Anquan Boldin with 2:43 left in the second tightened the contest to 10–7 at halftime.

Arizona tied the game with a Neil Rackers field goal after a 15-play drive to open the second half, then traded touchdowns with the Redskins to knot the game going into the fourth quarter. That's when the turnover bug struck again. Kurt Warner under-threw an open Steve Breaston, and the ball was tipped, picked off, and returned to the Arizona 15. Two plays later the Redskins scored what proved to be the game-winning touchdown.

Subsequent Washington miscues—a penalty that negated a long TD pass and a missed field goal—kept the Cardinals within striking distance, but they couldn't convert. Their last chance to tie the game, a drive starting on their own 42 with 3:23 remaining, ended with a punt after three ineffective plays. Kurt Warner's stats on the day were solid (16-of-30 for 192 yards and two touchdowns), but on this day the only numbers that really counted for him and the other Cards were the ones on the scoreboard. ∎

### FedEx Field (Landover, Md.)

| Final | 1 | 2 | 3 | 4 | T |
|---|---|---|---|---|---|
| Arizona (2-1-0) | 0 | 7 | 10 | 0 | 17 |
| Washington (2-1-0) | 7 | 3 | 7 | 7 | 24 |

### Game Leaders

ARI - Pass: K. Warner (16-30, 192), Rec: L. Fitzgerald (7-109)
WAS - Pass: J. Campbell (22-30, 193), Rec: S. Moss (7-75)

Head coach—and former Redskin—Ken Whisenhunt thought he tasted victory in the nation's capital, but was left with a bitter loss after the Redskins' fourth quarter comeback sent his team to its first defeat in 2008.

Adrian Wilson knocks down this Jason Campbell pass intended for Santana Moss. The Washington duo later connected for the game-winning touchdown.

# Game 4

## Warner and Favre face off in a QB duel for the ages

A much-anticipated battle between two long-in-the-tooth quarterbacks—Kurt Warner versus Brett Favre—turned out to be a mismatch in favor of the New York Jets and their recently unretired signal-caller. When the dust had settled at Giants Stadium after a game that saw 800-plus yards of total offense, the Arizona Cardinals found themselves on the short end of a 56–35 score.

In reality, the game wasn't nearly as close as the final tally suggested. Warner's stat line resounded with some heady numbers—40 of 57 passes for 472 yards and two touchdowns—but they don't tell the story of a second quarter in which he gave up two picks and two lost fumbles. Those mistakes led to a flurry of points and an insurmountable 34–0 lead for the Jets at halftime.

In the locker room, Arizona switched to the no-huddle offense and Warner put his first-half woes behind him. Three crisp third-quarter drives resulted in Cardinals' rushing touchdowns and pulled the visitors to within 34–21 at the start of the fourth quarter. The Jets, finally realizing that there was still some football to play, shook off their second-half funk and started matching the Cardinals touchdown-for-touchdown. The resulting score line was embarrassing for both teams' defenses and left Arizona with a 2–2 record and proof that more work needed to be done before the team started printing playoff tickets.

In throwing a career-high six touchdown passes, Favre seemingly sent a message to his former team, the Packers, that they should have welcomed him back after his short-lived retirement. Yet this game ended up being the high point of a disappointing season for Favre and the Jets. Meanwhile, for the old guy taking snaps for the Cardinals, this game was a relatively minor side trip on his magical ride back to the Super Bowl. ∎

### Giants Stadium (E. Rutherford, N.J.)

| Final | 1 | 2 | 3 | 4 | T |
|---|---|---|---|---|---|
| Arizona (2-2-0) | 0 | 0 | 21 | 14 | 35 |
| NY Jets (2-2-0) | 0 | 34 | 0 | 22 | 56 |

### Game Leaders

| | |
|---|---|
| ARI - Pass: K. Warner (40-57, 472), Rec: S. Breaston (9-122) | |
| NYJ - Pass: B. Favre (24-34, 289), Rec: L. Coles (8-105) | |

Overlooked after media darling Brett Favre's career day, Kurt Warner had a solid passing day himself at the Meadowlands. Though he threw three interceptions, he led the Cardinals comeback attempt and posted boffo fantasy numbers: 472 passing yards and two touchdowns.

Favre had the best
day of his Jets
tenure against the
Cardinals' defense.
He completed 24 of
34 passes, six of
which were touch-
downs.

# Game 5

## Cardinals rebound with a beat-down of the Bills

Looking to have a rebound game after their miserable seven-turnover performance at the Meadowlands against the Jets, the Cardinals returned home for a Week 5 inter-conference duel with the Buffalo Bills. The Cardinals took flight early in the first quarter as quarterback Kurt Warner completed a two-yard touchdown pass to Larry Fitzgerald. For their part, Buffalo suffered a key loss on just their third play of the game. After nearly sitting out the game, the Cardinals' Adrian Wilson ended up suiting up at the last minute, and his vicious hit on Bills quarterback Trent Edwards ended the passer's day early.

Less than a minute into the second quarter, Arizona increased its lead when sensational rookie Tim Hightower scampered into the end zone from 17 yards out. The Bills responded with backup quarterback J.P. Losman completing an 87-yard touchdown pass to speedster Lee Evans.

The Cardinals answered right back, capping their drive with a one-yard Edgerrin James touchdown run. Buffalo came right back downfield, with Losman carrying in from two yards out. The Cardinals managed to keep the momentum going into the half, as Neil Rackers connected with a 47-yard field goal as time expired.

In the third quarter, the Bills tried to mount a comeback as kicker Rian Lindell made a 48-yard field goal, but Arizona kept its intensity up as Warner completed another two-yard touchdown pass to Fitzgerald. In the fourth quarter, the Cardinals pulled away as Rackers nailed a 38-yard field goal and Hightower went back into the end zone from two yards out.

After his tough outing the week before at the Meadowlands, Kurt Warner completed 33 of 42 passes for 250 yards and two touchdowns. More importantly, he did not throw an interception and the Cardinals as a team had no turnovers.

"We're a tough team to beat when we don't turn the ball over," said coach Ken Whisenhunt. With the win, the Cardinals improved to 3–2. ∎

### University of Phoenix Stadium (Glendale, Ariz.)

| Final | 1 | 2 | 3 | 4 | T |
|---|---|---|---|---|---|
| Buffalo (4-1-0) | 0 | 14 | 3 | 0 | 17 |
| Arizona (3-2-0) | 7 | 17 | 7 | 10 | 41 |

### Game Leaders

BUF - Pass: J. Losman (15-21, 220), Rec: L. Evans (2-100)
ARI - Pass: K. Warner (33-42, 250), Rec: S. Breaston (7-77)

Adrian Wilson's jaw-crunching hit on the Bills' Trent Edwards came on the game's third play. Edwards was forced to leave the game, and J.P. Losman quarterbacked the Bills the rest of the way.

Running back Tim Hightower springs away from the Bills defense on his way to a 17-yard second-quarter touchdown. Hightower finished the day with 37 yards and two scores on seven carries.

# Game 6

## Cardinals shoot down Cowboys with a block that made history

Coming off their rout over the Bills and with confidence riding high, the Cardinals stayed at home for a crucial Week 6 showdown with the Dallas Cowboys. The Cardinals wasted literally no time in jumping out front, as J.J. Arrington—who had been inactive for the last four games—returned the opening kickoff 93 yards for a touchdown.

In the second quarter, the Cowboys tied the game when quarterback Tony Romo completed a 55-yard touchdown pass to receiver Patrick Crayton. The score remained tied heading into halftime.

Following the intermission, Dallas took the lead when Romo completed a 14-yard touchdown pass to Miles Austin. Arizona came back to tie the game with quarterback Kurt Warner completing a short two-yard touchdown pass to Larry Fitzgerald.

In the fourth quarter, the Cardinals regained the lead as Warner completed an 11-yard touchdown pass to Steve Breaston, followed by kicker Neil Rackers nailing a 41-yard field goal. The Cowboys managed to come back, and they tied the game when Romo completed a 70-yard touchdown pass to back Marion Barber and kicker Nick Folk drilled a 52-yard field goal, sending the game to an extra period.

In overtime, after forcing a three-and-out, Arizona got the win as wideout Sean Morey blocked a Mat McBriar punt attempt, allowing linebacker Monty Beisel to return it three easy yards for the game-winning touchdown. McBriar fractured his foot on the play and was put on injured reserve.

"I can't remember one that was this crazy," Arizona quarterback Kurt Warner said, "especially toward the end." It was the 423rd overtime game in NFL history, and the first that ended with a blocked punt being returned for a touchdown.

With the impressive win, the Cardinals entered their bye week at 4–2. They also were sitting at 3–0 at home. The start was their best since the 2002 season, when they finished 5–11. ∎

### University of Phoenix Stadium (Glendale, Ariz.)

| Final | 1 | 2 | 3 | 4 | OT | T |
|---|---|---|---|---|---|---|
| Dallas (4-2-0) | 0 | 7 | 7 | 10 | 0 | 24 |
| Arizona (4-2-0) | 7 | 0 | 7 | 10 | 6 | 30 |

### Game Leaders

DAL - Pass: T. Romo (24-38, 321), Rec: M. Barber (11-128)
ARI - Pass: K. Warner (22-30, 236), Rec: S. Breaston (8-102)

Larry Fitzgerald managed to hang on to this pass with one hand in the fourth quarter against the Cowboys. It was one of his five catches that were good for 79 yards and one touchdown.

The moment of impact: Sean Morey blocks Mat McBriar's punt before Monty Beisel scooped it up for the three-yard game-winning touch-down return. McBriar's foot was broken and he was placed on injured reserve.

# Game 7

## Second-half fade leaves Cardinals in the shadows

Coming off their bye week, the Cardinals flew to Charlotte's Bank of America Stadium for a Week 8 duel with the Carolina Panthers. It was a matchup of the NFL's two best rags-to-riches stories, as Kurt Warner faced the Panther's Jake Delhomme, who also had endured years of obscurity before becoming an NFL star. The two put on a quarterbacking clinic in their first head-to-head NFL meeting.

In the first quarter, the Cardinals jumped ahead by three points midway through the frame when kicker Neil Rackers converted a chip-shot 21-yard field goal. In the second quarter, Arizona increased its lead when quarterback Kurt Warner completed a five-yard touchdown pass to wide receiver Anquan Boldin, who ended up leading the Cardinals in rushing. The Panthers closed out the first half scoring when John Kasay converted from 23 yards out.

After the break, the Cardinals increased their lead as rookie Tim Hightower ran in from two yards out. Carolina began to rally, however, when running back DeAngelo Williams ran in from 15 yards, while Jake Delhomme completed an 18-yard touchdown pass to wideout Steve Smith.

The Cardinals replied with Warner hooking up with Boldin again on a two-yard touchdown pass, but the Panthers took the lead on Delhomme's 65-yard touchdown to Smith, who finished with 117 yards and two touchdowns. Carolina put the final icing on the cake in the fourth quarter when Kasay hit from 50 yards out.

With the tough loss, the Cardinals fell to 4–3. Delhomme managed to outduel Warner, though the Cardinals' passer still finished with 381 yards and two touchdowns with one interception. "We did a lot of good things," Warner said. "It's a good football team, but bottom line we made one too many mistakes." ∎

### Bank of America Stadium (Charlotte, N.C.)

| Final | 1 | 2 | 3 | 4 | T |
|---|---|---|---|---|---|
| Arizona (4-3-0) | 3 | 7 | 13 | 0 | 23 |
| Carolina (6-2-0) | 0 | 3 | 21 | 3 | 27 |

### Game Leaders

ARI - Pass: K. Warner (35-49, 381), Rec: L. Fitzgerald (7-115)
CAR - Pass: J. Delhomme (20-28, 248), Rec: S. Smith (5-117)

A disappointed Kurt Warner looks on during the matchup with the Panthers. Warner had a big day, throwing for 381 yards and two touchdowns, though the team fell just short.

Anquan Boldin celebrates after his third-quarter touchdown, his second of the day. The Cardinals missed the point after and gave the Panthers some inadvertent momentum.

# Game 8

## A triumphant return for a St. Louis legend

Looking for some medicine after the loss in Charlotte the week before, the Cardinals flew to the Edward Jones Dome for a Week 9 NFC West duel with the St. Louis Rams, who came into the game just 2–5. Returning to the field where he had led the Rams during two Super Bowl seasons and one championship, Kurt Warner was ready for a big game.

Arizona trailed early in the first quarter as Rams quarterback Marc Bulger—who was Warner's successor—completed an 80-yard touchdown pass to receiver Derek Stanley after the Rams had stopped the Cardinals' first drive. In the second quarter, the Cardinals took control as safety Antrel Rolle returned an interception 40 yards for a touchdown and kicker Neil Rackers made a 36-yard field goal. Tim Hightower got in on the fun with a 30-yard touchdown run, and Warner celebrated his return to St. Louis by completing a 56-yard touchdown pass to wide receiver Jerheme Urban. The 24-point explosion rendered the game all but over by halftime.

In the third quarter, the Cardinals continued their domination as Warner hit Anquan Boldin from seven yards out for another touchdown. In the fourth, St. Louis tried to rally as Bulger completed a three-yard touchdown pass to veteran Torry Holt. They were to get no closer, and Neil Rackers added a field goal to cap the scoring.

"A great day," said Warner, who finished 22-of-33 for 343 yards and two touchdowns. "I always love coming back to this place. Really a good day all the way around for me." With the win, the Cardinals improved to 5–3 while the Rams slipped further down the standings to 2–6. The next week, the Cardinals were to play in prime time on Monday Night Football against the division rival San Francisco 49ers. ∎

### Edward Jones Dome (St. Louis, Mo.)

| Final | 1 | 2 | 3 | 4 | T |
|---|---|---|---|---|---|
| Arizona (5-3-0) | 0 | 24 | 7 | 3 | 34 |
| St. Louis (2-6-0) | 7 | 0 | 0 | 6 | 13 |

### Game Leaders

| | |
|---|---|
| ARI - Pass: K. Warner (23-34, 342), Rush: T. Hightower (22-109) | |
| STL - Pass: M. Bulger (16-33, 186), Rec: D. Stanley (1-80) | |

Kurt Warner went back to work at his old stomping grounds in St. Louis. He torched the Rams secondary for 343 yards and two touchdowns, playing decidedly better than his successor in St. Louis, Marc Bulger.

J.J. Arrington tries to dance around the Rams defense. Arrington had a strong day out of the backfield, spelling Tim Hightower by rushing for 61 yards on seven carries.

# Game 9

## Guts and a goal-line stand lead to season sweep of 49ers

Coming off their divisional road win over the Rams, the Cardinals went home for a Week 10 NFC West rematch with the San Francisco 49ers on Monday Night Football. Confidence was running high, and the prime time experience had the players fired up.

The game did not start well for the Cardinals, however. San Francisco reserve cornerback Allen Rossum gave his team some early fireworks by returning the game's opening kickoff 104 yards for a touchdown. The Cardinals responded well as kicker Neil Rackers made a 28-yard field goal.

In the second quarter, however, San Francisco added to their lead when quarterback Shaun Hill hit wideout Josh Morgan for a 31-yard touchdown. The Cardinals answered with 10 straight points on a Warner-to-Boldin touchdown pass and another Rackers field goal. The 49ers were able to stretch their lead before the half, however, when Hill hit athletic tight end Vernon Davis with another touchdown pass.

After the break, Arizona crept closer again as Warner completed a five-yard touchdown pass to receiver Larry Fitzgerald, though San Francisco replied with kicker Joe Nedney converting a 41-yard field goal. In the fourth quarter, the Cardinals finally took the lead after Rackers nailed a 23-yard field goal, and Warner hooked up with Boldin again from five yards out. A failed two-point conversion, however, allowed San Francisco a chance to win.

The visitors drove down the field as the clock wound down and after a timeout called reserve wide receiver Michael Robinson's number. With star running back Frank Gore lined up as a wide out, Robinson—who played quarterback at Penn State—ran for the goal line. He was gang tackled by the Cardinals' defense short of the end zone and time ran out, preserving the win.

"We found a way to win a tough game, which is something you have to do," said coach Ken Whisenhunt, who stressed the win's positives. With the season sweep of the 49ers, the Cardinals improved to 6-3. ■

### University of Phoenix Stadium (Glendale, Ariz.)

| Final | 1 | 2 | 3 | 4 | T |
|---|---|---|---|---|---|
| San Francisco (2-7-0) | 7 | 14 | 3 | 0 | 24 |
| Arizona (6-3-0) | 3 | 10 | 7 | 9 | 29 |

### Game Leaders

SF - Pass: S. Hill (19-40, 217), Rush: F. Gore (23-99)

ARI - Pass: K. Warner (32-42, 328), Rec: S. Breaston (7-121)

Coach Ken Whisenhunt calls the defensive signals on Monday Night Football against the 49ers. The defensive unit proved to be critical, making a big stop to win the game.

The decisive play of the game: Time expires as the Cardinals stuff Michael Robinson from two yards out. The gang tackle followed a timeout where 49ers offensive coordinator Mike Martz decided to stick with his play call, thinking there was going to be a hole in the Cardinals defense.

# Game 10

## Cardinals get their kicks in stroll over Seahawks

Following their close call in the nail-biter against San Francisco on Monday Night Football, the Cardinals flew to Qwest Field for a Week 11 NFC West duel with the struggling Seattle Seahawks.

The Cardinals jumped ahead early, with kicker Neil Rackers hitting from 38 yards out and J.J. Arrington carrying in from four yards. In the second quarter, Arizona increased its lead to 13–0 when Rackers hit again, this time from 48 yards away. The Seahawks finally answered with quarterback Matt Hasselbeck completing a 13-yard touchdown pass to back Maurice Morris. The Cardinals pushed their lead back out to nine as time expired, however, when Rackers made a kick from 53 yards out.

As the second half opened, the Cardinals increased their lead when Rackers nailed a 26-yard field goal and Kurt Warner completed a six-yard touchdown pass to Arrington. It was the running back's second score of the day, a career best. He also led the Cardinals in rushing on the day with 40 yards.

Seattle furiously tried to rally in the fourth quarter as running back T.J. Duckett went in to the end zone twice from short range. Rookie cornerback Dominique Rodgers-Cromartie came up with a big play to seal the win, however, ending the Seahawks'

final rally with two minutes left thanks to a diving interception, his second of the day. With the victory, not only did the Cardinals win three straight for the first time since 2002, but they improved to 7–3 for the first time since 1977. They knew that the Seahawks four-year run at the top of the NFC was over and that they could clinch the NFC West with a win the next week.

"It was payback for what they did to us last year. They ran that score up," said Darnell Dockett of the Seahawks win in 2007. "That feeling, we all remembered that. That's going to be the best feeling in the world, winning the division. I've been here five years. Never won a division. Never won in Seattle." ■

### Qwest Field (Seattle, Wash.)

| Final | 1 | 2 | 3 | 4 | T |
|---|---|---|---|---|---|
| Arizona (7-3-0) | 10 | 6 | 10 | 0 | 26 |
| Seattle (2-8-0) | 0 | 7 | 0 | 13 | 20 |

### Game Leaders

ARI - Pass: K. Warner (32-44, 395), Rec: A. Boldin (13-186)
SEA - Pass: M. Hasselbeck (17-29, 170), Rec: D. Branch (4-54)

The Seahawks' Josh Wilson was unable to keep Larry Fitzgerald from catching this pass in the second quarter. Fitzgerald finished with 10 catches for 151 yards, which were, amazingly, the second-best receiving numbers among Arizona receivers in the game.

Kurt Warner had another vintage day calling the signals for the offense. He ended the day with a stunning 395 passing yards, 186 of which went to Anquan Boldin on 13 grabs.

# Game 11

## Giants reassert themselves as champions in the desert

After the pivotal road win in Seattle, the Cardinals went home for a Week 12 duel with the defending Super Bowl champions, the New York Giants. The Giants were excited to make their return to University of Phoenix Stadium, the site of their Super Bowl XLII win the previous season.

The Cardinals managed to jump ahead thanks to the only score of the first quarter, a 34-yard Neil Rackers field goal midway through the frame. The Giants responded in the second with running back Derrick Ward going into the end zone from one yard out. The Cardinals came right back, scoring just four minutes later on Tim Hightower's four-yard run.

The back-and-forth quarter continued as New York answered with kicker John Carney making a 33-yard field goal, putting New York in front 9–7. The Cardinals again replied with Neil Rackers, who converted a chip shot 20-yarder to put Arizona back in front. New York managed to close out the topsy-turvy quarter on top, however, when Super Bowl MVP Eli Manning hit Amani Toomer with a 12-yard touchdown pass with just over a minute to play.

In the third quarter, New York increased their lead as Manning completed a two-yard touchdown pass to fullback Madison Hedgecock. Arizona answered with Hightower running into the end zone from one yard out. In the fourth quarter, the Giants were starting to pull away after Manning completed a touchdown pass to tight end Kevin Boss, while Carney made a 27-yard field goal. The Cardinals tried to keep pace as Kurt Warner completed a five-yard touchdown pass to Anquan Boldin, but New York responded with a 33-yard Carney field goal. Arizona tried one last comeback attempt after Rackers made another field goal, but the ensuing onside kick failed and allowed New York to escape with a 37–29 win.

"They're a good defense and we matched up with them very well and went toe to toe with them for 60 minutes," said Kurt Warner, who finished with 351 yards passing despite being pressured for most of the game. "Of course, you never want to go away a loser and that part is disappointing. I think you leave from this game and move ahead. If we eliminate some of the mistakes we can play with anybody in the league." With the loss, the Cardinals fell to 7–4. ∎

**University of Phoenix Stadium (Glendale, Ariz.)**

| Final | 1 | 2 | 3 | 4 | T |
|---|---|---|---|---|---|
| NY Giants (10-1-0) | 0 | 17 | 7 | 13 | 37 |
| Arizona (7-4-0) | 3 | 9 | 7 | 10 | 29 |

**Game Leaders**

NYG - Pass: E. Manning (26-33, 240), Rush: D. Ward (20-69)
ARI - Pass: K. Warner (32-52, 351), Rec: A. Boldin (11-87)

Dominique Rogers-Cromartie defends against the Giants' Plaxico Burress. The receiver was knocked out of the game early with a hamstring injury, but it did not seem to hurt the Giants, who improved to 10-1 on the year.

Tim Hightower looks for daylight on his 55-yard kickoff return. The play set up Hightower's four-yard touchdown run that put the Cardinals up 9-7.

# Game 12

## Eagles carve up the Cardinals in Turkey Day tilt

Hoping to rebound on the road from their tough home loss to the Giants, the Cardinals flew to Lincoln Financial Field for a Thanksgiving Day battle with the Philadelphia Eagles. It was not a pretty performance.

Arizona trailed right from the get-go when Eagles quarterback Donovan McNabb completed a five-yard touchdown pass to star running back Brian Westbrook. Westbrook added a one-yard touchdown run later in the period.

In the second quarter, the Cardinals fell behind even further when McNabb hooked up with Westbrook again on a two-yard touchdown pass to push their lead to 21–0. The Cardinals finally responded as Kurt Warner completed a short one-yard touchdown pass to receiver Larry Fitzgerald, the first of his two touchdown receptions. Philadelphia added to their lead with just one second remaining in the half when David Akers connected from 42 yards out.

The Eagles pushed their lead to 31–7 right after the break when Westbrook carried into the end zone again. The Cardinals finally managed a response when Warner hooked up with Steve Breaston for an eight-yard touchdown. The Eagles quickly answered back on an Akers boot from 41 yards.

The Cardinals tried to rally in the fourth quarter when Warner connected with Fitzgerald again on a seven-yard touchdown pass. But Philadelphia managed to seal their win with two straight scores, as McNabb hit wideouts DeSean Jackson and Jason Avant with short touchdown strikes to push the final score to 48–20.

"It sure seemed like we came out flat," Arizona coach Ken Whisenhunt said of the Cardinals' slow start. "I don't know if we were mentally prepared. We played hard, but obviously made too many mistakes. We weren't as crisp as we had been."

Others were not thrilled with the loss either. "It's not the game we wanted to play," Warner said. "I came out and forced one early. We just didn't have our game today and it was across the board." The Cardinals fell to 7–5 with the loss. ∎

### Lincoln Financial Field (Philadelphia, Pa.)

| Final | 1 | 2 | 3 | 4 | T |
|---|---|---|---|---|---|
| Arizona (7-5-0) | 0 | 7 | 6 | 7 | 20 |
| Philadelphia (6-5-1) | 14 | 10 | 10 | 14 | 48 |

### Game Leaders

ARI - Pass: K. Warner (21-39, 235), Rec: L. Fitzgerald (5-65)
PHI - Pass: D. McNabb (27-39, 260), Rush: B. Westbrook (22-110)

The Philadelphia defense allowed J.J. Arrington and the other Cardinals backs no running room. Arrington led all Arizona rushers, but went for just 10 yards on a pair of carries.

Larry Fitzgerald leaps to make a catch in front of Philadelphia's Lito Sheppard. Fitzgerald was one of the brightest spots on the Arizona offense, catching five passes for 65 yards and a pair of touchdowns.

# Game 13

## Cardinals clinch division crown by smashing the Rams

Rebounding quickly from their road woes, the Cardinals dominated St. Louis for the second time in 2008 to win the NFC West and clinch their first home playoff game since 1947's NFL Championship Game at Comiskey Park.

Arizona took a 14–0 lead in the first quarter and never looked back after a one-yard Tim Hightower touchdown run was followed by 12-yard scoring strike from Kurt Warner to Larry Fitzgerald. The Rams tried to close the gap in the second quarter after a Warner interception led to a Marc Bulger touchdown pass.

The Cardinals responded by increasing their lead again thanks to two field goals from Neil Rackers to make the halftime score 20–7. In the third quarter Cardinals linebacker Gerald Hayes forced a pair of Steven Jackson fumbles—the second one was recovered by Darnell Dockett, who lumbered 11 yards into the end zone for a touchdown.

Down 27–7, the Rams tried to rally after a long field goal pulled them to within 17 points, but a Bulger pass was intercepted by rookie cornerback Dominique Rodgers-Cromartie, who ran it back 99 happy yards for the touchdown that sealed the game. The win propelled the Cardinals to their first playoff game since 1998 and their first division title since the days the Cardinals were in St. Louis in 1975. The celebration was on in Arizona.

The Cardinals were not sure how to celebrate their win, reacting with joy after dousing Ken Whisenhunt with Gatorade. "My coach was like, 'Act like you've been there before, act like you've been there before,'" said an elated Darnell Dockett. "I said 'Coach, I ain't been there before. I don't know how to act right now.'"

With the win, the Cardinals record improved to 8–5 and they were looking to close the season out strong heading into the playoffs. ∎

### University of Phoenix Stadium (Glendale, Ariz.)

| Final | 1 | 2 | 3 | 4 | T |
|---|---|---|---|---|---|
| St. Louis (2-11-0) | 0 | 7 | 0 | 3 | 10 |
| Arizona (8-5-0) | 14 | 6 | 7 | 7 | 34 |

### Game Leaders

| |
|---|
| STL - Pass: M. Bulger (22-37, 228), Rush: S. Jackson (19-64) |
| ARI - Pass: K. Warner (24-33, 279), Rec: S. Breaston (7-90) |

Kurt Warner heads up the tunnel celebrating the Cardinals' division title. Fittingly, it came after another strong performance against his former team, the Rams, against whom he completed 24 of 33 passes for 279 yards and a touchdown.

Darnell Dockett celebrates the touchdown that put the game away. His 11-yard fumble return for a score was the Cardinals' first of two defensive touchdowns and put the team up 27-7.

# Game 14

## Cardinals flight halted with a sudden thud in Minnesota

Locked in a duel with the Minnesota Vikings for the third seed in the NFC playoffs, the Week 15 matchup with the NFC North leaders was of vital importance to the Cardinals. Unfortunately, things looked bleak for the Cardinals from the beginning, despite playing against a relatively inexperienced quarterback.

The Vikings started the scoring with an 82-yard punt return touchdown by the speedy Bernard Berrian. Two turnovers from the Cardinals, a Kurt Warner interception, and an Anquan Boldin fumble, led to two touchdown passes from Tarvaris Jackson. The quarterback, who had been benched at the start of the year for aging veteran Gus Frerotte, first connected on a 41-yard pass to the slippery Berrian and followed with a 19-yard pass to Sidney Rice.

The Vikings continued their dominance in the Cardinals' home stadium and took a 28–0 lead at halftime after an 11-yard touchdown pass from Jackson to running back Chester Taylor. The Cardinals managed to rally and cut the lead in half in the third quarter with a Jerheme Urban 50-yard touchdown catch and a field goal blocked by Dominique Rodgers-Cromartie that was recovered by Roderick Hood, who returned it 68-yards

for a touchdown. It was the last highlight of the day for the Cardinals.

The Vikings managed to pull away for good at the end of the third quarter when Jackson threw a 59-yard touchdown pass to Bobby Wade. It was Jackson's fourth touchdown pass of the day, an unlikely result from the backup quarterback of a team known for its rushing assault.

"It appeared to me in the game that we did not come out ready to play," Ken Whisenhunt said, obviously displeased with the team's second poor outing in three weeks. "That's something we had concerns about because we hadn't handled success that well in the past."

With the loss, the Cardinals dropped to 8–6 and looked to finish the season strong with two games to play. ■

### University of Phoenix Stadium (Glendale, Ariz.)

| Final | 1 | 2 | 3 | 4 | T |
|---|---|---|---|---|---|
| Minnesota (9-5-0) | 21 | 7 | 7 | 0 | 35 |
| Arizona (8-6-0) | 0 | 0 | 14 | 0 | 14 |

### Game Leaders

MIN - Pass: T. Jackson (11-17, 163), Rush: A. Peterson (28-165)
ARI - Pass: K. Warner (29-45, 270), Rec: J. Urban (3-82)

Defensive tackle Gabe Wilson looks on in the final minutes of the loss to the Vikings. The line struggled to contain the Minnesota rushing attack and allowed the Vikings to run for 239 yards on the day.

Minnesota speedster Bernard Berrian runs by Ben Graham on his 82-yard punt-return touchdown in the first quarter. It was the first score of the game and for Berrian, who also caught a 41-yard touchdown pass from Tarvaris Jackson.

# Game 15

## Snowy conditions cause concern for crushed Cardinals

Hoping to rebound from their home loss to the Vikings, the Cardinals flew to wintry Gillette Stadium for a Week 16 inter-conference duel with the New England Patriots. It was ugly from the get-go for the desert-dwelling NFC West champions. The Patriots, hungry to keep their playoff hopes alive, dominated from the opening kickoff in what turned out to be a laugher.

Arizona trailed early in the first quarter, and indeed never led or tied the game again after Patriots running back LaMont Jordan ran in twice from short yardage to put the home side up 14–0. The Cardinals' East Coast struggles continued in the second quarter as quarterback Matt Cassel completed a 15-yard touchdown pass to running back Kevin Faulk and an 11-yard touchdown pass to wide receiver Wes Welker. Kicker Stephen Gostkowski's 38-yard field goal capped off a first half that finished 31–0, meaning that the Cardinals had been outscored in the first half 59–0 over the last two games.

Things did not improve for the Cardinals in the second half. Cassel completed a 76-yard touchdown pass to wide receiver Randy Moss while Gostkowski added a pair of short field goals to push the Patriots advantage to 44–0. In the fourth quarter, New England concluded its domination of the Cardinals with Gostkowski's 30-yard field goal.

The Cardinals finally got on the board with a meaningless touchdown as quarterback Matt Leinart–who had come off the bench to replace Kurt Warner in the third quarter—completed a 78-yard touchdown pass to wide receiver Larry Fitzgerald. Leinart played well in relief, throwing for 138 yards with a score and an interception.

With the loss, Arizona fell to 8–7. They were understandably frustrated about the poor performance. "Right now, we aren't what we were," said Warner, who only completed six passes for 30 yards in the snowy conditions. "If we're happy with winning the division, then that's all we'll do."

The loss seemed to do some good, as the Cardinals were to come out ready to play in the season's final week. ■

### Gillette Stadium (Foxborough, Mass.)

| Final | 1 | 2 | 3 | 4 | T |
|---|---|---|---|---|---|
| Arizona (8-7-0) | 0 | 0 | 0 | 7 | 7 |
| New England (10-5-0) | 14 | 17 | 13 | 3 | 47 |

**Game Leaders**

| |
|---|
| ARI - Pass: M. Leinart (6-14, 138), Rec: L. Fitzgerald (3-101) |
| NE - Pass: M. Cassel (20-36, 345), Rec: J. Gaffney (5-90) |

A stunned Ken Whisenhunt looks on through the snow in the closing minutes of the Cardinals' lopsided loss to the Patriots. New England kept its playoff hopes alive with the 47–7 thumping of the visitors, but they ultimately missed out on the postseason.

Kurt Warner and the offense were never able to get in gear due to the weather in Foxborough and a hungry New England defense. Warner threw for just 30 yards in one of the worst games of his professional career. Matt Leinart managed 138 yards passing in relief, including the Cardinals' only score.

# Game 16

## Cardinals recapture momentum for the playoffs

Following some weak and worrisome performances in December, the Cardinals went home for a Week 17 NFC West rematch with the Seattle Seahawks looking to close the regular season on a high note. After previously ending the Seahawks' four-year reign of dominance atop the NFC West, the Cardinals were also looking to complete a season sweep of their rivals.

The game did not start well for Arizona, as they trailed early in the first quarter after Seahawks' running back T.J. Duckett found the end zone from one yard out. The Cardinals managed to respond in the second quarter when quarterback Kurt Warner completed a 16-yard touchdown pass to wide receiver Jerheme Urban and a five-yard touchdown pass to wide receiver Larry Fitzgerald to take a 14–7 lead. Seattle did manage to tie the game at halftime with backup quarterback and reserve wide receiver Seneca Wallace, who completed a 30-yard touchdown pass to wide receiver Deion Branch.

Arizona pushed back out in front midway through the third quarter when Warner completed a 38-yard touchdown pass to Fitzgerald. Seven minutes later, he completed a 14-yard touchdown pass to wide receiver Steve Breaston, which extended the lead to 28–14. Seattle tried to rally in the fourth quarter when Wallace completed a second touchdown pass to Branch, but the Cardinals were able to close out the game when kicker Neil Rackers hit a pair of short field goals to help seal a 34–21 win.

With the victory, the Cardinals closed out the regular season at 9–7. "Somewhere in the second quarter we woke up and we played like the Cardinals," Arizona coach Ken Whisenhunt said, "and that was nice to see."

The coach was clearly pleased with the strong finish to the regular season. He and his team were ready for the Atlanta Falcons and the NFC Playoffs. ∎

### University of Phoenix Stadium (Glendale, Ariz.)

| Final | 1 | 2 | 3 | 4 | T |
|---|---|---|---|---|---|
| Seattle (4-12-0) | 7 | 7 | 0 | 7 | 21 |
| Arizona (9-7-0) | 0 | 14 | 14 | 6 | 34 |

**Game Leaders**

SEA - Pass: S. Wallace (24-43, 250), Rec: D. Branch (6-90)
ARI - Pass: K. Warner (19-30, 263), Rec: L. Fitzgerald (5-130)

Larry Fitzgerald seemingly had glue on his hands in the Week 17 win over the Seahawks. This score went for 38 yards and was one of two touchdowns by Fitzgerald in a 130-yard performance.

Seattle's Will Herring felt the full brunt of Edgerrin James' stiff arm on this play. James showed that he was ready for the playoffs with his 14-carry, 100-yard performance on the regular season's final day.

# Kurt Warner: The Early Years

## His unlikely journey from small-town Iowa to the NFL

### By Gary Ronberg

Kurt Warner grew up in the Iowa heartland, near the rapids of the Cedar River, where the first European settlers were farmers from Germany, Czechoslovakia, Austria, and Poland who raised oats and corn and wheat in what would become the breadbasket of America. They would be followed later by waves of immigrants from England and Scotland, Norway and Sweden, who embraced and augmented the values of their predecessors.

They all brought with them the values and customs of the Old Country, while evolving into fiercely proud Americans, Iowans, and fellow citizens. They believed in self-reliance and hard work, in God and country, in traditions, respect for community, and church bells on Sunday. They waved at friends and strangers alike through the windshields of their cars and trucks, from the swing or chair on the front porch.

"People in Iowa are terrific, friendly everywhere you go," Warner says. "So many places today, you can walk down the street, say hello, and nobody really answers you. In Iowa, you can start a conversation by saying hello."

When he was four years old, Warner's mother, Sue, a homemaker, and his father, Gene, divorced. Kurt and his older brother, Matt, lived with their mother and spent every other weekend with their father. Both parents tried hard to make the lives of their sons as normal and fruitful as possible. Sue began working for a company in town that manufactured plastic bags. She was strong, strict, and loving, and her boys responded as young gentlemen, with enduring affection and respect. Gene continued to be a good father, arranging his Saturdays and Sundays around the things fathers and sons commonly do together. When he remarried, he brought the son of his new wife, Mimi, into the lives of his own children. The boy's name also was Matt, like Kurt's older brother. Soon all three were brothers in every way.

"The boys became very close," says Gene. "They have become wonderful young men, responsible, caring, sons to be proud of."

Mimi's Matt agrees, "There was never any stepbrother stuff. We were brothers from the start. We are and always will be."

The boys' world revolved around sports, which helped keep a broken family from falling apart altogether. Matt Warner was more into music, but when Kurt had a ball—a basketball, football, or baseball—he was captivated. Kurt's first love was basketball, but football was a close second.

*After a successful career at Cedar Rapids' Regis High School, Kurt Warner found himself buried on the depth chart at Northern Iowa. It wasn't the last time Warner would be underestimated by coaches.*

The boys and their friends would play football and baseball in the cemetery for hours. A family in the neighborhood, the Larimers, had a large meadow for their backyard and permitted the boys to take a lawn mower and dress it up with sidelines, yard-line stripes, the works. As they played, they imagined themselves in the yellow, black, and white of the Iowa Hawkeyes, playing in Big Ten games against Illinois, Wisconsin, Michigan, and Michigan State. Then, on Sundays, they would play for the Dallas Cowboys, the Green Bay Packers, and Los Angeles Rams. "From Friday after school to Sunday night, we were there," remembers step-brother Matt. "In the back of one of our end zones was a vegetable garden. If we had a difference of opinion, some tomatoes flew."

Matt and Kurt Warner would mature beyond their years, particularly after their mother divorced a second time. The three of them lived from pay-check to paycheck, and from this hardship came dedication to honest labor, diligence, and self-motivation. Matt worked in the produce depart-ment of a grocery store; Kurt labored in the fields, where he detasseled corn in the summer. They were good students and well-behaved; getting into trouble was not an option.

High school sports are big in Cedar Rapids. At Regis High School, then a small Catholic school of about 400 students, Kurt's maturity and competitive spirit established him as a leader. He earned All-State honors in basketball and football. "Kurt has a unique confidence in himself," says Gene Warner. "He isn't afraid of responsibility and pressure."

Despite his achievements on the basketball court, Kurt knew he wasn't tall or fast enough to attract a basketball scholarship to college. He pinned his hopes on football, and in the fall of his senior year he received an invitation from Iowa head coach Hayden Fry to attend a Hawkeyes game at Kinnick Stadium. He was elated. His mother and a friend accompanied him to Iowa City where they were given a tour of the stadium and introduced to some of the players on the field before the game. But Coach Fry did not speak to him after the Hawkeyes defeated Northwestern and Kurt returned home, crushed. "It hurt," he recalls. "It hurt bad. I was probably the best quarterback in the state, and he never even shook my hand."

The state's only other major college, Iowa State, did not bother to write or call him at all; their coaches wanted a running quarterback, not a passer. The lone scholarship offer came from the University of Northern Iowa in Cedar Falls, where Warner was told he could compete for the starting quarterback position after being red-shirted for a year. Once on campus, however, Warner found himself behind a quarterback a year ahead of him who was good enough to keep the position throughout his college career. Bottom line: he would patrol the sidelines for four seasons.

Those years (1989–1992) were long and diffi-cult, particularly when some of his teammates and

When Warner was finally given the chance to start at Northern Iowa, he made the most of his opportunity. He threw for more than 300 yards four times and was named the Gateway Conference's Offensive Player of the Year.

Though he put up impressive numbers in his lone season as a starter, Warner spent most of his time at the UNI Dome on the bench, learning and building character. Considered the best quarterback in Iowa coming out of high school, Warner was understandably frustrated at not getting a chance to earn the starting job.

Both Brett Favre and Warner know what it's like to be passed over. Favre was a castoff in Atlanta before the Packers made him a superstar. Warner briefly served as an understudy of Favre when he was signed by Green Bay as an undrafted free agent.

coaches were convinced that he should at least have been playing, if not starting. "All I wanted was a chance to compete for starting quarterback," he says.

It would be an appeal he would echo throughout his football career.

He thought about quitting the team and playing basketball, but the football coaches would hear nothing of that. He considered transferring to another college. His parents told him to stay at Northern Iowa and concentrate on his degree. After all, a diploma was more important than football anyway. His mother told him that his experience was building character. "Mother," he replied, "I have enough character. I don't need any more character."

When his senior year finally arrived, he made the most of it on the football field. He led the Gateway Conference in total offense and passing yards. In four of his games, he threw for more than 300 yards. He quarterbacked Northern Iowa to the conference championship and into the Division I-AA playoffs. Twice he was Gateway's Player of the Week. At season's end he was its Offensive Player of the Year.

After this stellar season, he bumped into Hayden Fry at a few sports banquets where the Iowa coach appeared to delight in telling audiences how he'd missed the chance to make him a Hawkeye. Fry later tried to make up for his oversight by inviting him to work out for National Football League scouts at Kinnick Stadium. Warner would later spend two long days at home in

front of the TV, watching the draft and waiting for a phone call that never came. "Rejection had become a pattern," his father recalls. "The beauty of it is, Kurt never gave up on himself."

He probably should have faced up to it right then and there, just stashed the nightmare that his dreams had become and moved on with the rest of his life. After all, he'd gotten his communications degree at Northern Iowa. He'd been an honor student in high school and college. He was smart and gracious. People liked him. He was prepared for the real world.

But he didn't. When a chance came to sign with an NFL team as an undrafted free agent, the Green Bay Packers and San Diego Chargers each offered him $5,000. He chose the Packers and was flown out to their mini-camp in Arizona where a limousine driver met his plane, carried his bags, and squired him to a very nice hotel.

All too soon, however, he discovered he had much to learn—and no time to learn it. So intricate was the Green Bay attack, and he had no clue. One afternoon, after quarterback coach Steve Mariucci asked him to run a particular play, Warner declined to even enter the team's huddle. He simply did not know what he was supposed to do. There were already three very good quarterbacks on the field— Brett Favre, a future Hall of Famer; Mark Brunell, soon-to-be All-Pro at Jacksonville, and Ty Detmer, the Heisman Trophy winner from Brigham Young.

By the time Green Bay's training camp opened

Kurt's wife, Brenda, has been one of his most vocal supporters. A former Marine and a divorcee with two children when she met Warner, the two have formed a special bond.

in August at St. Norbert College in Wisconsin, Warner was primed. His throwing was crisp, sharp, and he knew the Packers playbook inside out. He looked good in Packers green and yellow. He felt professional too, like this was the way it's supposed to be. He devoured information in the quarterback meeting and relished instruction on the practice field. Complex as they were, he knew all the passing lanes, the timing of the receivers' routes and breaks. All the homework he'd done since the mini-camp was paying off.

The other three quarterbacks were good guys, too. Brett called him Chachi, after Fonzie's cousin on TV's *Happy Days*. Mark and Ty called him

"Pop," as in the Pop Warner League. Mariucci was "Mooch," and the two are friends to this day. The problem was, the other three ran the team in practice and the exhibition games while he stood and watched. In six weeks, he ran exactly 12 plays in camp and was ignored in two games. Then the phone rang in his dorm room. "Come downstairs. Bring your playbook." Only Favre would stay. Warner was cut, Brunell and Detmer would be traded. Said Mariucci, "All four did well. It just took a little longer for Kurt to show what he could do."

For the first time he began to wonder if he'd make it. He viewed his Packers experience with optimism. He had demonstrated the ability to

(above) Brenda and Kurt have stood by each other through thick and thin and have enjoyed the life that football has given them, while giving back whenever they can. (opposite) There were many lows early in Warner's career. There was the time spent as an assistant at Northern Iowa while working at a local Hy-Vee food store, along with successful stints in the Arena Football League and NFL Europe.

absorb an intricate, demanding offense. He knew how to run it. He'd long ago mastered his field skills and leadership capabilities. Today Mariucci, who went on to become head coach of the San Francisco 49ers [and the Detroit Lions], says St. Norbert College in August of 1994 simply was neither the place nor the time for Kurt Warner. The Packers had three fine quarterbacks. All had professional experience. Each was making a lot of money. None was about to carry a clipboard and be on the phone to the coaches upstairs while Kurt Warner tried to prove himself on the field. "Now I understand what Mooch meant when he said I wasn't ready back then," Warner says. "I only had a year of college experience. It would have been difficult to step in and perform as I would later. As it turned out, I needed my experiences of the next five years to perform the way I can now."

———————————————

There she was, voted All-American cheerleader her senior year in high school, seeking direction and excitement, discipline and maturity, an ultimate sense of accomplishment—in other words, a wondrous adventure, an open door to the world, an opportunity to broaden her horizons, and to enhance her development as a woman.

Naturally, she chose the United States Marine Corps.

"My parents couldn't afford college for my sister very easily and I knew they wouldn't be able to afford things for me," she recalls. "I had heard their struggles about money. So I signed up with the U.S. Marines with their signatures because I was so young."

At the age of 17, two weeks after graduating from high school, Brenda Carney Meoni left all her friends in Cedar Rapids for Marine boot camp at Parris Island, South Carolina.

Today she reveres her years as a Marine, the demands that were made of her, the challenges that brought forth strengths she may never have known she possessed. The rewards flowed in so many ways, from her bearing and self-confidence to the very feel and texture of the uniform she wore so proudly. "I was able to send money back to my parents. I still miss the people, the camaraderie of the Marine Corps, the knowledge that every day everybody would be at work, ready to go." She pauses in reflection. "Today, I hear people who skip an appointment say, 'I didn't feel like going.' And I say to myself, 'How can you not?'"

At the age of 25, she was a mother of two, divorced, and living with her parents. From Parris Island she had become a Marine Corporal based in Virginia near the nation's capital, specializing in intelligence. She had married a Marine and given birth to their first child four months earlier when her phone rang at work. It was her husband, and he told her their baby boy, Zachary, had stopped breathing in the bathtub. She rushed home, they gathered up Zachary, and rushed him to the hospital emergency

Warner tasted his first professional success with the Iowa Barnstormers. He led the team to two Arena Bowl appearances and was All-Arena in both 1996 and 1997. He was later named to the list of the 20 best players in league history.

room a block away. After a battery of tests, the doctors still could not determine why the baby's brain kept swelling. The next day her husband admitted he'd accidentally dropped Zachary in the bathtub, bumping the back of his head. This was terrible news; it explained the trauma in the rear of Zachary's brain.

The doctors said it was unlikely their son would survive, and that even if he did, he would be blind with no chance at a normal life. Oh, how Brenda prayed. Her prayers got her through the despair of Zack's days and weeks in the hospital, through his violent seizures and illnesses, and even the fears and anger she harbored. Zachary lived, but when he displayed no signs of improvement, the doctors said they could do no more for him suggested he be taken home.

Brenda took an honorable discharge from the Marine Corps and she, her husband, and Zack moved back to Iowa. Within a year their marriage unraveled. She took Zack and moved into her parents' home in Cedar Falls, filing for divorce a month before giving birth to a baby daughter, Jesse Jo. She enrolled in nursing school and hoped to make a better life for her children.

Her father, Larry Carney, worked for John Deere. Her mother, Jenny Joe, was a homemaker, and they lived in a modest two-bedroom home on Simeon Street. When she arrived with her babies, the house became cramped and chaotic. Two years later, when her boyfriend, Kurt, moved in, the four

of them moved downstairs to a basement with a lamp or two, a few spiderwebs, and the cold. There wasn't room anywhere else.

Although Larry and Jenny Joe Carney welcomed Kurt Warner into their home, he was embarrassed to live there. He had a degree from the local university, but his dogged pursuit of a pro football career had left him with no job, no money, and no future in the NFL. He had been cut by the Green Bay Packers and auditioned for the Cincinnati Bengals, Tampa Bay Buccaneers, and Atlanta Falcons—all to no avail. There was a sense among family and friends that he should give up his fantasy and get on with the rest of his life. "We were living on her food stamps and the aid Brenda was getting for college," he says. "It was not the way I wanted to take care of her and the children."

They had met at Wild E. Coyote's, a country-and-western club near the Northern Iowa campus. He was in his third year on the sidelines for the football team. A teammate had taken him to the bar to cheer him up. She had gone to the place a few times with friends and had even taken line-dancing lessons there after her mother suggested it might be a good idea for her to get out of the house now and then. They had noticed each other before.

"I saw this lady on the dance floor constantly, dancing with every guy in the place," he recalls.

"I thought it took a lot for a man to come and ask a woman to dance, and if someone got up the nerve to ask me I would say yes," she says. "I do

During their unlikely odyssey through football, Kurt and Brenda's bond grew stronger and they found Jesus. Active born-again Christians to this day, they both strive to emulate Jesus' example of love and kindness.

remember this good-looking guy, and he always had a whole bunch of people around him. They all happened to be female, usually," Carney said.

After their first night on the dance floor, she made sure he knew everything about her. She was divorced, the mother of two, and lived with her parents. "If I never hear from you again," she said, "I'll understand." At 9:00 the next morning the door bell rang and there he was with a rose in his hand.

He said he wanted to meet the children. "I was real protective of my kids," she says. "I wouldn't let guys meet my kids."

She pauses at the memory. "For whatever reason, something inside me said to let him meet them. I really pray about what I consider the Spirit talking to me, and in Kurtis's case, I just felt like, 'Go with it.' So he's on the floor and wrestling with Zachary, and I didn't even have time to explain that my son has brain damage and he's blind."

He was 21 and found her different from the rest. She was savvy, definitive, structured. "She had a background, was more interesting, was a little bit older. Maybe I'd matured more in growing up, and I needed someone on that level."

She sensed that too. "I broke up with a guy to go out with Kurtis. The man I broke up with was a special-needs teacher from a strong family, a Catholic background. He lived in Cedar Falls. Into my life comes this 21-year-old football star and who knew what was going to happen? If I had been looking for a father [for my children], I wouldn't have picked a young football star. He was just different. Better than anyone I'd ever dreamed of. I thought my life would be better if I stayed with him, just because of the kind of person he is."

They had no money, so their dates mainly amounted to playing with Zack and Jesse Jo. Their families and friends couldn't figure out the relationship, but they were intrigued by his sudden transition from college youth to family man. "He would come over, we'd order Domino's Pizza for $9.00, and wrestle on the floor with the kids and maybe watch a movie. And he'd go home. That was our date. I mean, real cheap."

After being cut by the Packers, he kept his professional football hopes flickering by practicing a few hours each day at Northern Iowa. The rest of the time he took care of Zack and Jesse Jo while Carney attended Hawkeye Community College. To bring in some money, he went to work for $5.50 an hour on the night shift at the Hy-Vee, a nearby 24-hour supermarket. "It was important for me to understand that some things are more important than professional football," Warner said.

Given his local celebrity, working at the supermarket was a humbling experience. Here was the star quarterback at the university with a degree in communications who had been rejected by four pro football teams. Now he was wearing a blue shirt with the tag that read, "Hello, my name is Kurt." He stocked shelves, swept floors, cleaned up spilled applesauce and broken jars, bagged groceries,

Warner knew he was ready for the NFL after a successful season with NFL Europe's Amsterdam Admirals. He led the league in touchdowns and passing yards.

**114**

walked customers to their cars, and put their bags in the trunk. He was never ridiculed, but he did sense what people might be saying over the backyard fences. "I had surrendered whatever pride I had left."

It had been six months at the Hy-Vee, before the guys from the fledgling Arena Football League came calling. They were starting up a team called the Iowa Barnstormers two hours away in Des Moines. He was a bankable football commodity throughout the state, and they wanted to talk. He had caught a few of their games on television in the early morning hours, nodding off on the couch, It wasn't quite what he had in mind for his career in football.

It wasn't 80,000-seat stadiums, network TV, and million-dollar contracts. There were no chartered jets and pristine practice fields and state-of-the-art weight rooms. This was Barnum & Bailey circus football in indoor arenas on artificial carpets half the length of a normal field, with eight players on a team instead of 11. Players ran all over the place and into each other, thudding off padded walls and occasionally tumbling over them into the laps of the specatators. This was pigskin-spiraling, high-fiving, end zone–juking football with the full array of promotional gimmickry, halftime contests, thundering music, and roaring announcers. And, hopefully, a sufficient number of fans would turn out and pay to watch players like him, guys who couldn't make it in the NFL.

But in March of 1995, he was in no position to be selective. He was 24 years old, working the late shift at a supermarket earning minimum wage and living with his girlfriend, her parents, and her two kids. With the Barnstormers he could make a $1,000 a game instead of $41 a night. He signed with the team, moved to Des Moines, and after struggling at first with the cramped playing fields and pinball nature of the game, he developed a feel for indoor football. In three seasons he raided defenders with all the spirals the league desired and more, striking for 10,486 yards and 183 touchdowns. He became the Arena League's highest-paid player at $60,000, not to mention a celebrity around Des Moines. They called him "Houdini" Warner because of his ducking and weaving, squirming and spinning from grasps and lunges, all the chaos culminating with still another of his magical throws.

On the Sunday night of April 14, 1996, he was watching television at his apartment in Des Moines. He'd played in an exhibition the night before in Moline, Illinois, and was just nodding off about midnight when the phone rang. It was Brenda, calling from Cedar Falls. "Mom and Dad were killed in a tornado. I need you." Click.

He called back once. Twice. Three times. The line was busy.

A week earlier, Larry and Jenny Joe Carney had moved into the dream home they had built on the White River in Arkansas. That Saturday had

The passing motion that has made Warner famous: He rode his wave of success into 1999 with an MVP season to go along with his Super Bowl title and Super Bowl MVP honors. Many were stunned by his rise from obscurity, including *Sports Illustrated*, who put his picture on the cover with the caption, "Who IS this guy?"

been Larry's 54th birthday, and Brenda had last talked to her father on Sunday afternoon. He mentioned tornado warnings in the area—not unusual for that time of the year—and that Jenny Joe had a headache. He said they planned to go to their new church that night to be baptized and would call her when they returned home. When the phone rang at 10:00 PM, she assumed it was her parents calling as promised. Instead it was her sister, Kim, with the worst possible news.

That evening the Carneys had stayed home because of Jenny Joe's headache. About 7:30 PM, two tornadoes collided above them. They didn't have a chance. Their home was destroyed. Five neighbors also were killed. All that remained was devastation and heartbreak. Brenda was a devout evangelical Christian, but the deaths of her father and mother shook her to her soul, to the very core of her belief in God.

She had been "born again" at age 12. During a Sunday night service at Sunny Side Temple in Waterloo, Iowa, she had risen from the pew and walked down to the altar to pray for forgiveness and ask Jesus to come into her heart. "I was saved that night," she said.

Kurt Warner was raised a Catholic. He attended Mass every Sunday and tried to be a good Christian and follow the Ten Commandments. He believed that if he was a good person, if he helped others, and praised the Lord with his heart and mind, he had a shot at heaven. Her view was not so

accommodating. She told him he had to have a personal relationship with the Lord and that he must first ask Jesus into his life. Quoting scripture, she insisted that no person earns salvation through good works, that all are sinners, that the only way to be saved is through God's grace. "Your salvation is a gift from God," she said. "Just ask Him. He will save you from Hell. Jesus is your friend. He's here. You need him in your life every minute of every day."

Their disagreements grew heated. She was unyielding in her belief that he still wasn't saved. He was just as convinced that his religious beliefs were personal, between him and his God, and quite frankly, they were none of her business. She said that if he had devoted his life to Christ, he would be out there telling people about Him. He perceived that as implication that he wasn't a Christian at all. "I didn't want to hear it. I didn't want any part of it. I still felt the way I was raised, and what I believed in, was enough."

Playing for the Barnstormers, he lived two hours away. One of his teammates had started up a Bible group with a local pastor and he began to attend their meetings. There would be no single moment when he felt he was born again, as Carney believed she had been. It was a gradual process for him, one that had originated in Des Moines and evolved over a span of months. He did not tell her or anyone in Bible group about the prayers he offered up for his salvation.

With his career seemingly over after a rough stint in New York, the Arizona Cardinals gave Warner a shot as a free agent. After star draft pick Matt Leinart fizzled, coach Ken Whisenhunt had the courage to give the starting reins to Warner, and together they led the Cardinals to their first-ever Super Bowl.

It was during the days and weeks following her desperate call to Des Moines that he sensed his life changing. He had threw on some clothes that night and sped to Cedar Falls so fast he could have been pulled over anywhere along on the highway. When he walked through the door, he found her distraught, among friends and neighbors.

He became her rock. He kept his own hurt from her because she hurt so deeply herself. He took care of Zack and Jesse Jo. He tried to answer their questions about what had happened to Grandpa and Grandma. "I really began to feel the Lord's presence in my life," he says. "I could just feel His peace all over me."

The stark irony was that as he began to believe as she did, she was beginning to question her faith. Her father and mother? Swept away, never to be seen alive by her again? How possibly could this have happened to them?

"I don't have the answers to why my parents were killed," she said. "I could either go through it and not love God, or go through it and love God. I don't understand why they died, but I know that He still loves me and that someday maybe it will make sense. Maybe it will be in Heaven when I ask Him. I also know I've got things to do here, so I can't stay in that 'Why me?'"

He did not use words to try to help her through her grief. There were no lame attempts to explain or rationalize. He just listened and tried to absorb some of her pain and anger, to comfort her, espe-

cially after what had happened to her son four years earlier. "He didn't preach to me. He just listened. He held me. He was quiet and strong. That's what I needed."

Her parents' remains were cremated, and after the memorial service she, her sister, brother-in-law, and Warner stood in the parking lot of a Baptist church in Mountain View, Arkansas. They were about to drive to her father's favorite fishing hole on the White River to scatter the ashes when she braced him. "You know, if you don't marry me it's stupid that you're even here." A few hours later, on the banks of the river, she raised her concerns again. They'd known each other for four years. They'd been through so much together. What was next? Were they or were they not a couple? "I'll always have this memory of you being here at this time. But are you somebody I'll know in 10 years?"

He knew she wasn't being unreasonable, that she deserved an answer. In the wake of her tragic loss, life in fact loomed even more precious to him now. He realized he needed to spend as much of his life as he could with her and her children. "We belong together," he told her. A few weeks later, she and her children moved to his apartment in Des Moines. They were engaged in September, and a year later they were married.

It was a beautiful wedding, with more than 250 friends and family in attendance. It was difficult without her father to escort her down the aisle and her mother missing from the front pew, but it was

Warner arrives with his teammates on the tarmac in Tampa. The elder statesman of the Cardinals, Warner told his teammates after the NFC Championship Game to enjoy every minute of the buildup to the Super Bowl, but to not get distracted by the parties.

joyful for them and the children. "I think the one thing that connected Kurtis and me was the moment he lay down on the floor and wrestled with Zachary the first time he visited us. Kurtis wasn't scared of him. It didn't matter to him that his eyes were crossed and he couldn't see. When Zachary was a baby, everywhere we'd go I'd hear comments like, 'Oh-h-h-h! What's wrong with him?' Other kids would always be looking at him. And people were making these judgments about my beautiful son!"

By 1997, Warner's boffo numbers in the Arena league had attracted interest from NFL Europe, a training ground for aspiring NFL players. He was interested, but now, after leading the Barnstormers to a 12–2 record and a second-straight berth in the league championship game, just married and living in a new home, he was not about to risk a future headed for the six figures. He put out the word that if an NFL team would sign him to a contract, and sponsor him in Europe, he would go. Only the St. Louis Rams, under the direction of head coach Dick Vermeil, bit.

When his European season unfurled with the Amsterdam Admirals, Warner quickly showed his stuff with dazzling performances against the Rhein Fire, the Scottish Claymores, and the Barcelona Dragons. He injured his ribs in Spain, and while he was sidelined he was surprised by a visit from Brenda and the children. She was not bringing good news. A pap smear from the early stages of her pregnancy had produced a provisional diagnosis of cervical cancer, and nothing could be confirmed until after their baby was born. "The men of the Bible study group who had led Kurtis to the Lord collected money and sent me and the kids over there so I could tell him face-to-face," she said. Thankfully, the threat was erased upon the birth of Kade, their first child together.

"Amsterdam was about as different as it got for a guy from Iowa," Warner says, "but the thing that was most familiar to me was an outdoor field, 100 yards long. I was finally back in real football."

As a cosmopolitan center of Europe with myriad temptations, the Dutch metropolis offered all sorts of distractions, many of which Warner faced when he had to walk through the red light district on his way to church. "I just gave my life over to Him and said, 'You take me, You lead me, You help me,'" he said. "That's when I really saw what He could do about temptations. It's been that way ever since."

In his nine starts for the Admirals, Warner led the league with 2,101 yards passing, 326 attempts, 165 completions, and 15 touchdowns. This was of no surprise to Charley Armey, the Rams' new general manager and former director of player personnel. It was Armey who, acting on the tip of a trusted friend, Amsterdam coach Al Luginbill, had lobbied Vermeil to fund Warner in Europe. Carefully tracking Warner's play, Armey then flew to Amsterdam, watched the quarterback at work, took him to dinner, then returned to St. Louis con-

The crush of Media Day can be stressful on players, but Warner handled his third appearance with class. With his unlikely return to football's biggest state, he was the center of attention among Cardinals players and displayed the eloquence and thoughtfulness that earned him a captain's patch.

vinced he had found the team's backup quarter-back, or at the very least, third string. Even so, Armey says, "I had to fight for a year and a half to keep Kurt Warner on our roster."

Armey was convinced that indoor football's hectic nature had honed Warner's precision and accuracy under pressure. His throws seemed to draw receivers to them, like a magnet; players did not have to speed up, slow down, or reach back to catch a ball from Warner, whether it was one cra-dled from 50 yards away or one that left a vapor trail at 20. Armey also believed his arena experi-ence had "slowed down" the conventional game for Warner, greatly increasing his poise, reads, timing, and accuracy.

Ten days after Warner returned from Europe, the Rams opened training camp. Every other rookie on the roster had been through two mini-camps and become familiar with the St. Louis play-book and lingo. Though impressed by Warner's accuracy, Vermeil found him lacking in knowledge of the system. The night before the final cut, Vermeil was still torn between Warner and Will Furrer, who knew the system. It wasn't until the 11th hour that he chose Warner.

---

Warner's story once he reached the NFL is now familiar to many fans. Serving as the Rams' backup QB in 1998, Warner took over the starting job in 1999 after a preseason injury sidelined Trent Green. Warner responded by throwing for 4,353 yards and 41 touchdowns, earning the NFL MVP award, and leading the Rams to victory in Super Bowl XXXIV, a game in which he was named the MVP. A broken hand shortened Warner's 2000 season, but he rebounded nicely in 2001, earning his second MVP and leading St. Louis to another Super Bowl, this time a close loss to the Patriots. Warner had cemented his reputation as an elite NFL quarterback.

Then things began to unravel. In 2002 a bro-ken finger seemed to affect both Warner's throwing ability and his confidence. In 2003 he was benched in favor of Mark Bulger. In June 2004 the Rams released Warner. It was a stunning fall from the top.

New York was Warner's next stop, but his time there did little to resurrect his career. Warner was clearly a stopgap QB for the Giants while highly touted rookie Eli Manning learned the ropes. Manning eventually replaced Warner in 2004's tenth game, and his short stint in New York was soon over. Warner's shooting-star career seemed to be burning out—until the Arizona Cardinals offered him one more chance. Much to delight of Cardinals' fans, it was an opportunity that Warner made the most of during the remarkable 2008 season. ∎

One of the most popular players at Media Day, Warner sat for questions until time ran out. Gracious with the reporters and thankful for the chance to play in another Super Bowl, Warner was ready for another championship performance.

# Kurt Warner NFL Stats

## Passing

| Year | Team | G | GS | Att | Comp | Pct | Yds | YPA | Lg | TD | Int | Sacked | 20+ | 40+ | Rating |
|------|------|---|----|----|------|-----|-----|-----|----|----|-----|--------|-----|-----|--------|
| 1998 | St. Louis Rams | 1 | 0 | 11 | 4 | 36.4 | 39 | 3.55 | 21 | 0 | 0 | 0/0 | 1 | 0 | 47.2 |
| 1999 | St. Louis Rams | 16 | 16 | 499 | 325 | 65.1 | 4353 | 8.72 | 75 | 41 | 13 | 29/201 | 60 | 16 | 109.2 |
| 2000 | St. Louis Rams | 11 | 11 | 347 | 235 | 67.7 | 3429 | 9.88 | 85 | 21 | 18 | 20/115 | 49 | 14 | 98.3 |
| 2001 | St. Louis Rams | 16 | 16 | 546 | 375 | 68.7 | 4830 | 8.85 | 65 | 36 | 22 | 38/233 | 81 | 11 | 101.4 |
| 2002 | St. Louis Rams | 7 | 6 | 220 | 144 | 65.5 | 1431 | 6.50 | 43 | 3 | 11 | 21/130 | 15 | 1 | 67.4 |
| 2003 | St. Louis Rams | 2 | 1 | 65 | 38 | 58.5 | 365 | 5.62 | 37 | 1 | 1 | 6/38 | 3 | 0 | 72.9 |
| 2004 | New York Giants | 10 | 9 | 277 | 174 | 62.8 | 2054 | 7.42 | 62 | 6 | 4 | 39/196 | 24 | 6 | 86.5 |
| 2005 | Arizona Cardinals | 10 | 10 | 375 | 242 | 64.5 | 2713 | 7.23 | 63 | 11 | 9 | 23/158 | 37 | 4 | 85.8 |
| 2006 | Arizona Cardinals | 6 | 5 | 168 | 108 | 64.3 | 1377 | 8.20 | 64 | 6 | 5 | 14/104 | 15 | 5 | 89.3 |
| 2007 | Arizona Cardinals | 14 | 11 | 451 | 281 | 62.3 | 3417 | 7.58 | 62 | 27 | 17 | 20/140 | 44 | 5 | 89.8 |
| 2008 | Arizona Cardinals | 16 | 16 | 598 | 401 | 67.1 | 4583 | 7.66 | 79 | 30 | 14 | 26/182 | 50 | 12 | 96.9 |
| TOTAL | | 109 | 101 | 3557 | 2327 | 65.4 | 28591 | 8.04 | 85 | 182 | 114 | 236/1497 | 379 | 74 | 93.8 |

## Career Highlights through the 2008 Regular Season

- By doing it in just his 36th career game, he reached 10,000 passing yards sooner than any other player in NFL history

- Has 48 career 300-yard passing games, including five in a row in 2008, and four 400-yard passing games

- A two-time NFL MVP (1999 and 2001); was also named Super Bowl XXXIV MVP after leading the Rams to a victory over the Tennessee Titans (1/30/00)

- Has posted a perfect passer rating of 158.3 three times (10/1/00 vs. SD; 10/3/99 @ Cin and 9/14/08 vs. Mia); became the first player in NFL history to record two "perfect" games with a minimum of 20 passes attempted

- A four-time Pro Bowler, he has led the NFL in passing yardage, completion percentage, and average gain per attempt three times each; has had the highest quarterback rating; and led the league in touchdown passes twice

- Career completion percentage of 65.4% ranks #2 in NFL history

- His career QB rating of 93.8 ranks #3 in NFL history behind only Steve Young (96.8) and Peyton Manning (94.7)

Kurt Warner throws a pass during practice on January 28, 2009, before Super Bowl XLIII in Tampa.

Kurt Warner signs a T-shirt for a fan as a boy walks away after getting Warner's autograph following a morning practice on January 31, 2009, prior to Super Bowl XLIII in Tampa.

TRIUMPH
BOOKS